**nickelodeon**™

降去神通

# AVATAR

## THE LAST AIRBENDER™

Created by
**Bryan Konietzko**
**Michael Dante DiMartino**

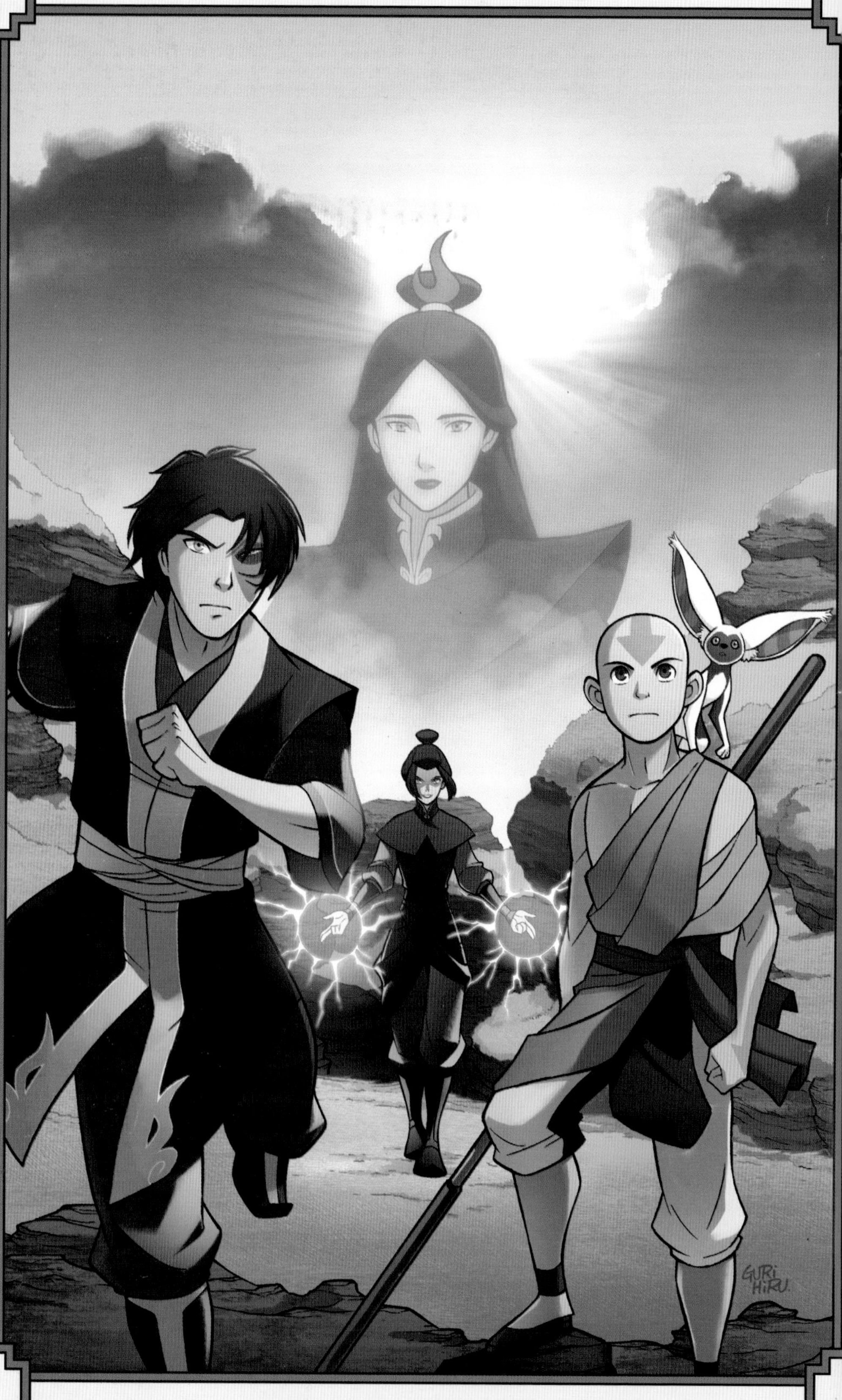
GURI HIRU.

# nickelodeon™

降击神通

# AVATAR

## THE LAST AIRBENDER™

THE SEARCH · PART ONE

script
**GENE LUEN YANG**

art and cover
**GURIHIRU**

lettering
**MICHAEL HEISLER**

**DARK HORSE BOOKS**

publisher
**MIKE RICHARDSON**

collection designer
**JUSTIN COUCH**

assistant editors
**SHANTEL LAROCQUE** and **IAN TUCKER**

editor
**DAVE MARSHALL**

Nickelodeon Avatar: The Last Airbender™—The Search Part 1

Special thanks to Linda Lee, Kat van Dam, James Salerno, and Joan Hilty at Nickelodeon, and to Bryan Konietzko and Michael Dante DiMartino.

Published by
**Dark Horse Books**
A division of
Dark Horse Comics, Inc.
10956 SE Main Street
Milwaukie, OR 97222

DarkHorse.com
Nick.com

To find a comics shop in your area, call the Comic Shop Locator Service toll-free at (888) 266-4226.

First edition: March 2013
ISBN 978-1-61655-054-7

5 7 9 10 8 6

Printed in China.

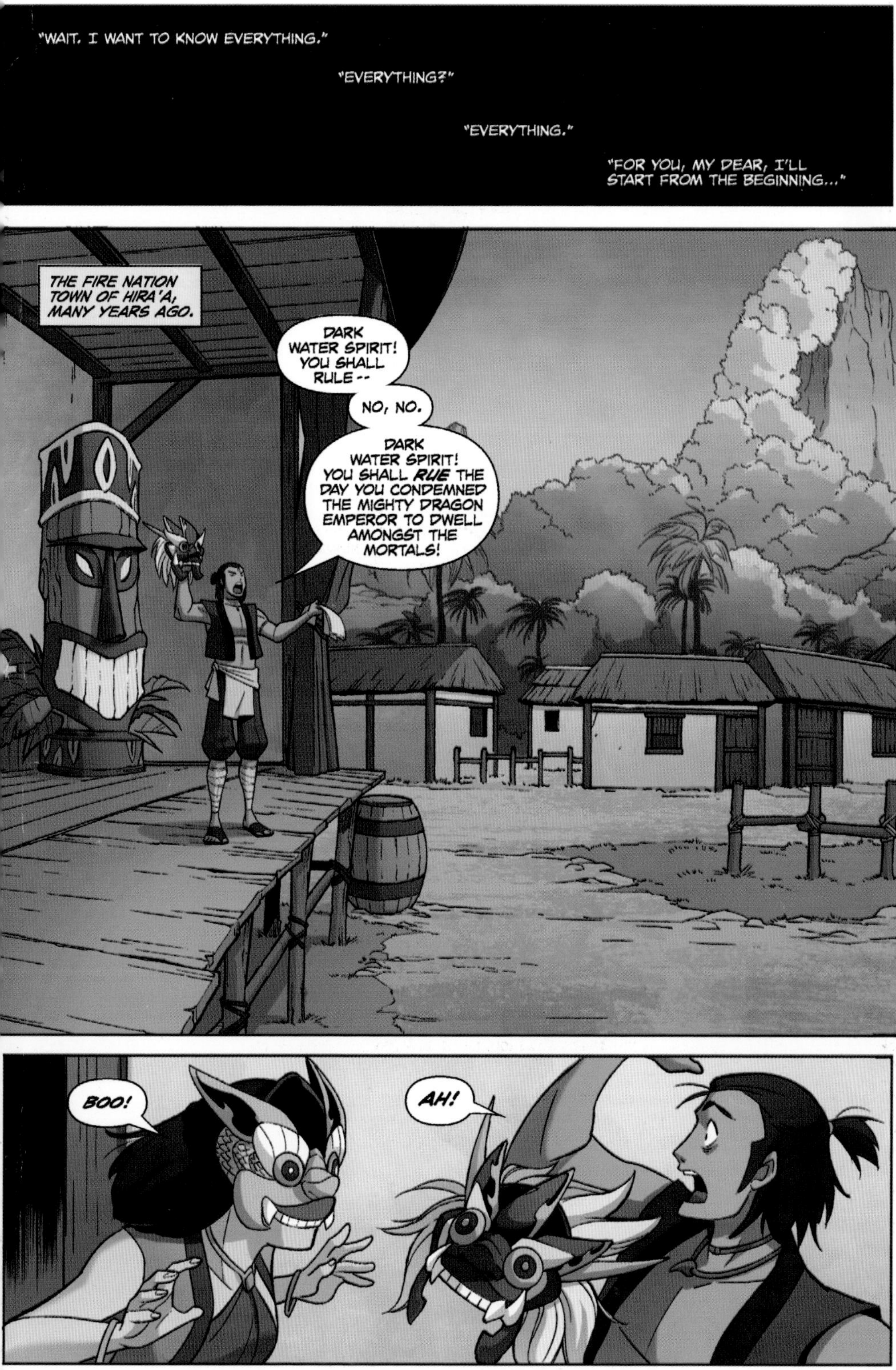
"WAIT. I WANT TO KNOW EVERYTHING."
"EVERYTHING?"
"EVERYTHING."
"FOR YOU, MY DEAR, I'LL START FROM THE BEGINNING..."
THE FIRE NATION TOWN OF HIRA'A, MANY YEARS AGO.
DARK WATER SPIRIT! YOU SHALL RULE --
NO, NO.
DARK WATER SPIRIT! YOU SHALL RUE THE DAY YOU CONDEMNED THE MIGHTY DRAGON EMPEROR TO DWELL AMONGST THE MORTALS!
BOO!
AH!

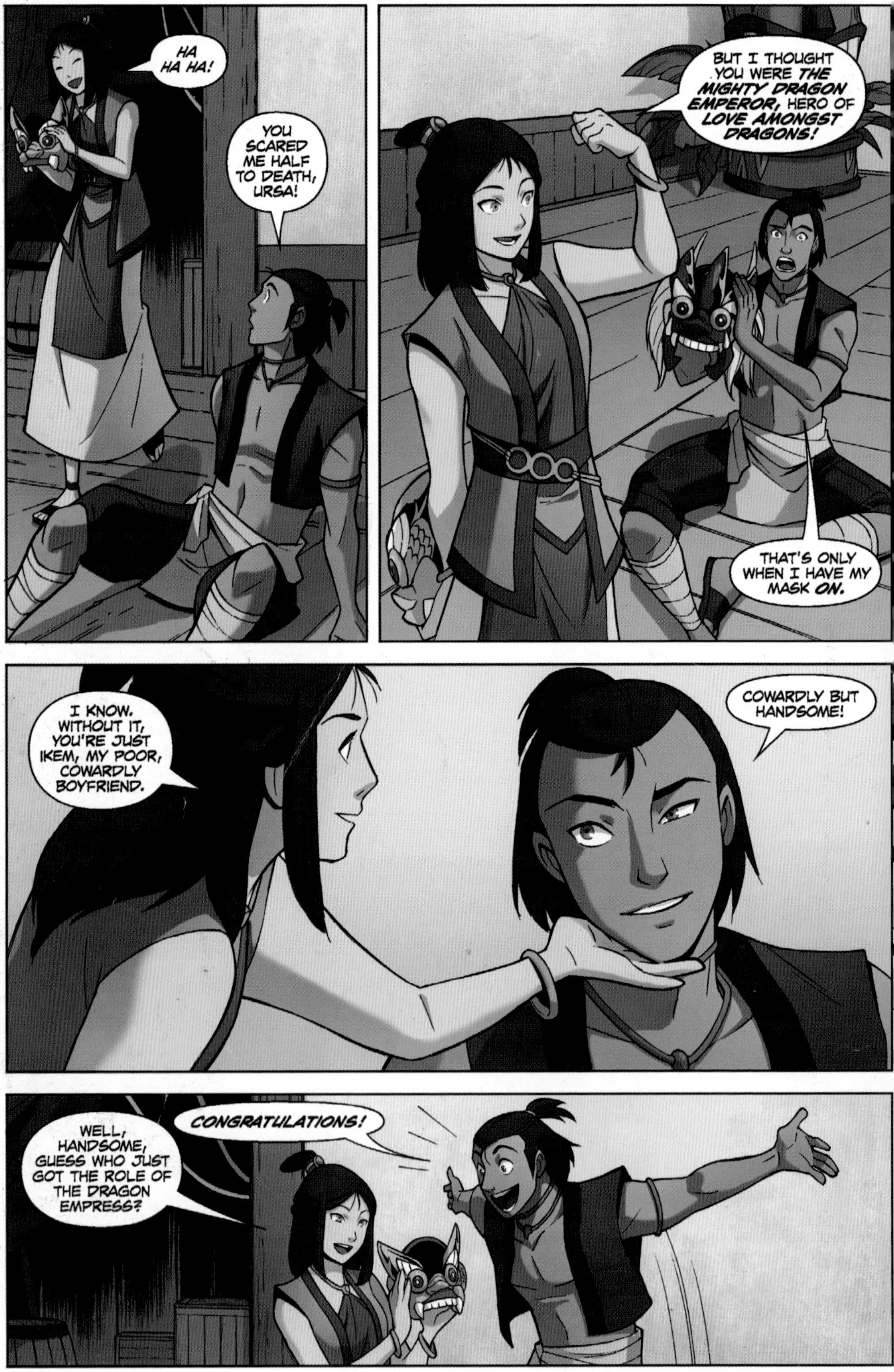
HA HA HA!
YOU SCARED ME HALF TO DEATH, URSA!
BUT I THOUGHT YOU WERE THE MIGHTY DRAGON EMPEROR, HERO OF LOVE AMONGST DRAGONS!
THAT'S ONLY WHEN I HAVE MY MASK ON.
I KNOW. WITHOUT IT, YOU'RE JUST IKEM, MY POOR, COWARDLY BOYFRIEND.
COWARDLY BUT HANDSOME!
WELL, HANDSOME, GUESS WHO JUST GOT THE ROLE OF THE DRAGON EMPRESS?
CONGRATULATIONS!

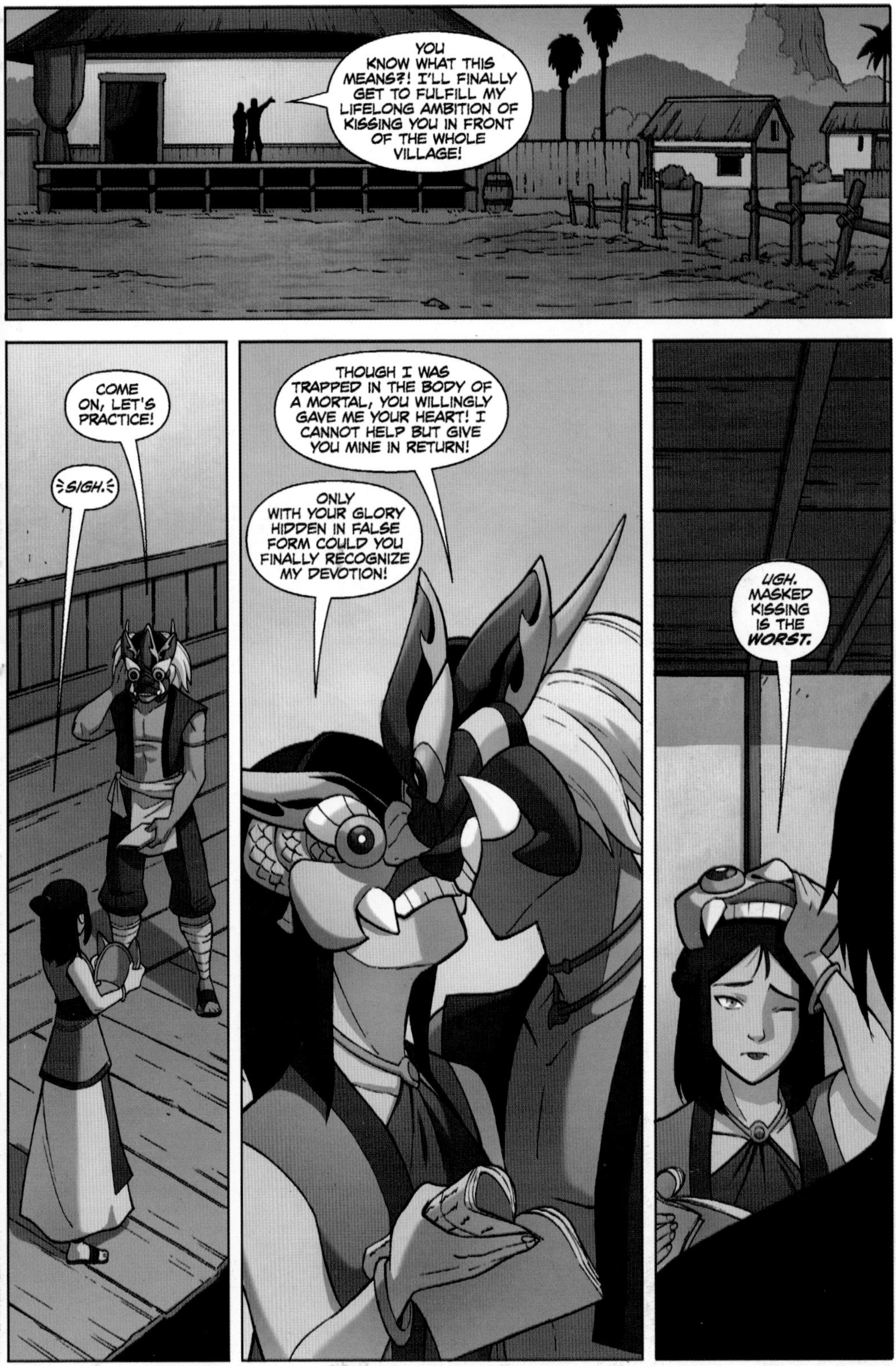
YOU KNOW WHAT THIS MEANS?! I'LL FINALLY GET TO FULFILL MY LIFELONG AMBITION OF KISSING YOU IN FRONT OF THE WHOLE VILLAGE!
COME ON, LET'S PRACTICE!
SIGH.
THOUGH I WAS TRAPPED IN THE BODY OF A MORTAL, YOU WILLINGLY GAVE ME YOUR HEART! I CANNOT HELP BUT GIVE YOU MINE IN RETURN!
ONLY WITH YOUR GLORY HIDDEN IN FALSE FORM COULD YOU FINALLY RECOGNIZE MY DEVOTION!
UGH. MASKED KISSING IS THE WORST.

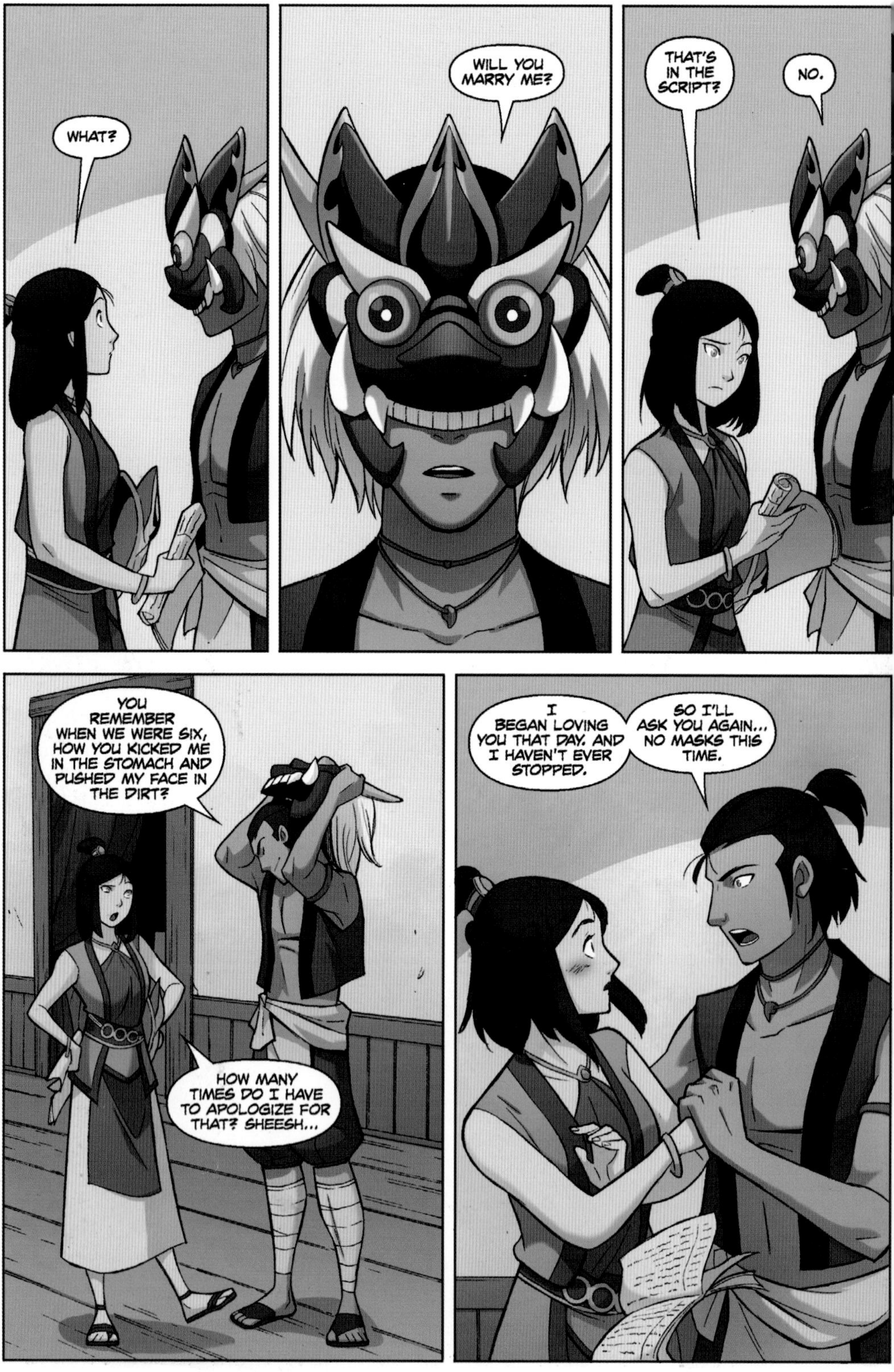
WHAT?
WILL YOU MARRY ME?
THAT'S IN THE SCRIPT?
NO.
YOU REMEMBER WHEN WE WERE SIX, HOW YOU KICKED ME IN THE STOMACH AND PUSHED MY FACE IN THE DIRT?
HOW MANY TIMES DO I HAVE TO APOLOGIZE FOR THAT? SHEESH...
I BEGAN LOVING YOU THAT DAY. AND I HAVEN'T EVER STOPPED.
SO I'LL ASK YOU AGAIN... NO MASKS THIS TIME.

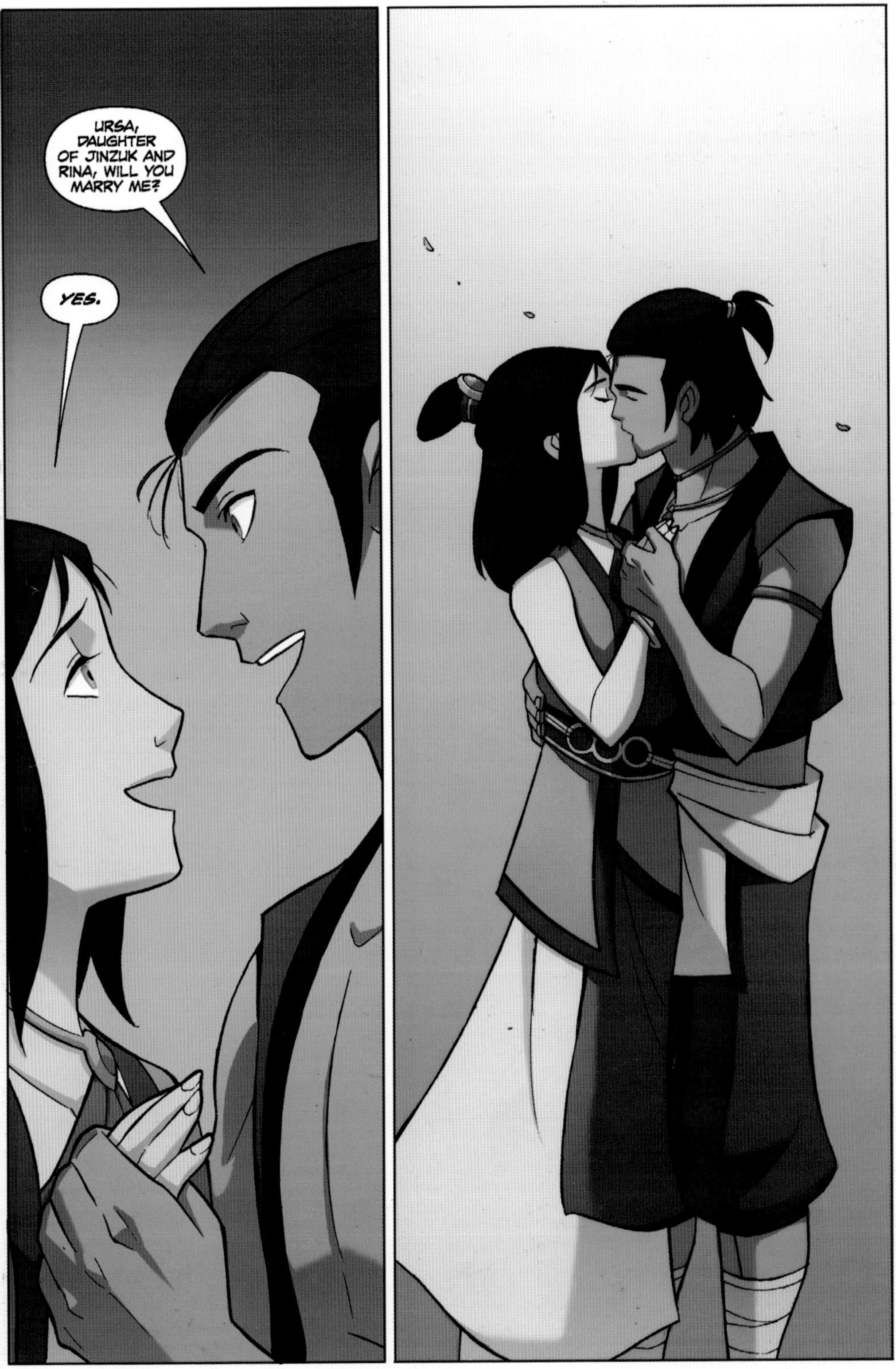
URSA, DAUGHTER OF JINZUK AND RINA, WILL YOU MARRY ME?
YES.

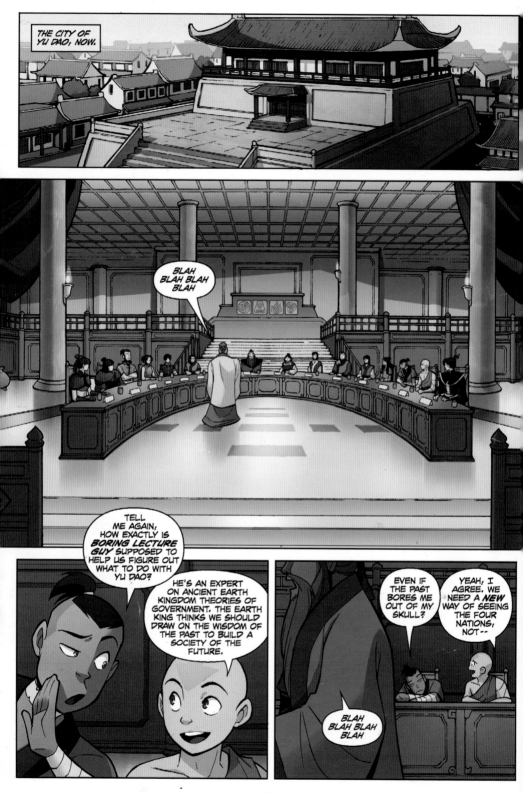

THE CITY OF YU DAO, NOW.

BLAH BLAH BLAH BLAH

TELL ME AGAIN, HOW EXACTLY IS *BORING LECTURE GUY* SUPPOSED TO HELP US FIGURE OUT WHAT TO DO WITH YU DAO?

HE'S AN EXPERT ON ANCIENT EARTH KINGDOM THEORIES OF GOVERNMENT. THE EARTH KING THINKS WE SHOULD DRAW ON THE WISDOM OF THE PAST TO BUILD A SOCIETY OF THE FUTURE.

EVEN IF THE PAST BORES ME OUT OF MY SKULL?

YEAH, I AGREE. WE NEED A *NEW* WAY OF SEEING THE FOUR NATIONS, NOT--

BLAH BLAH BLAH BLAH

10

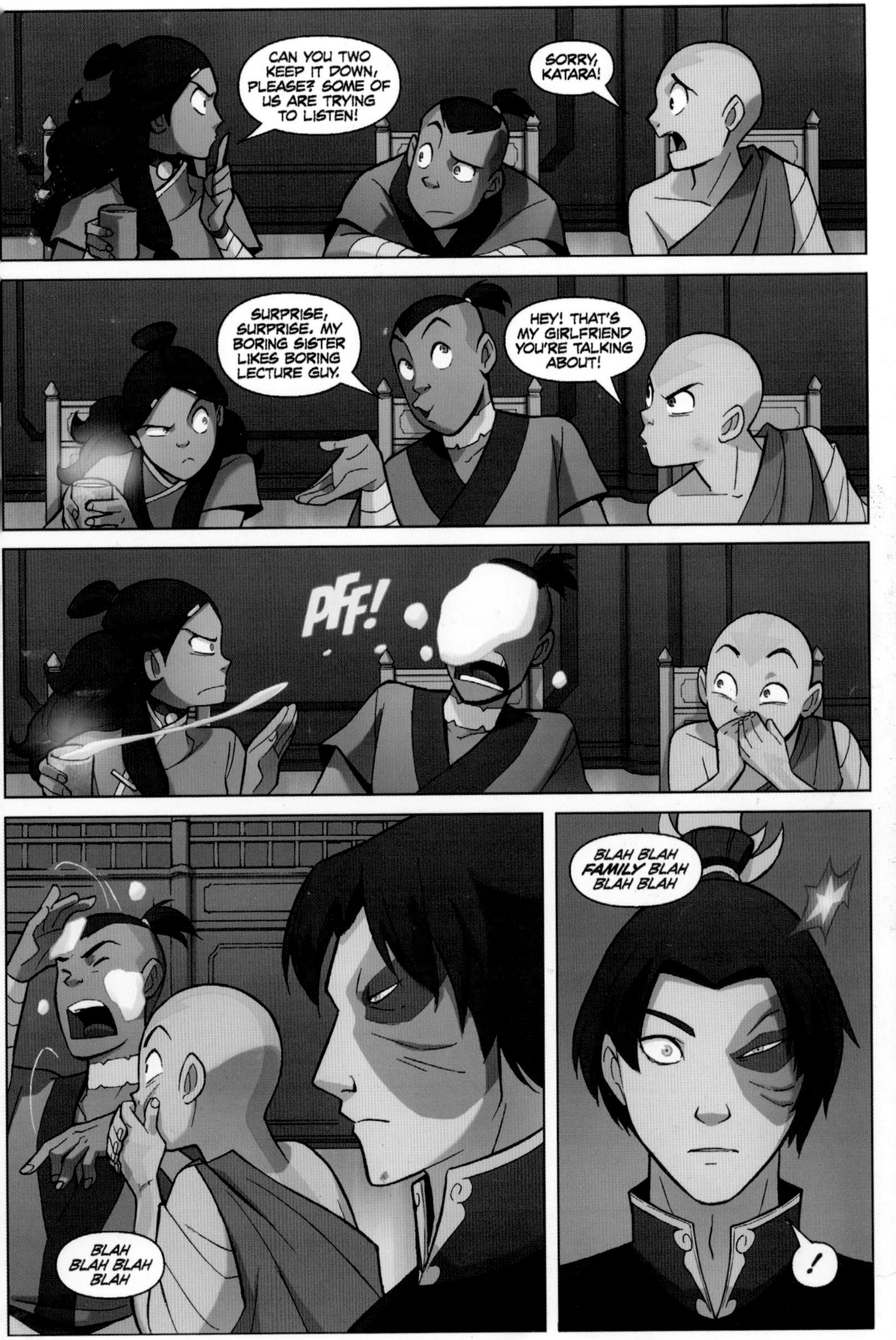
CAN YOU TWO KEEP IT DOWN, PLEASE? SOME OF US ARE TRYING TO LISTEN!
SORRY, KATARA!
SURPRISE, SURPRISE. MY BORING SISTER LIKES BORING LECTURE GUY.
HEY! THAT'S MY GIRLFRIEND YOU'RE TALKING ABOUT!
PFF!
BLAH BLAH BLAH BLAH
BLAH BLAH FAMILY BLAH BLAH BLAH
!

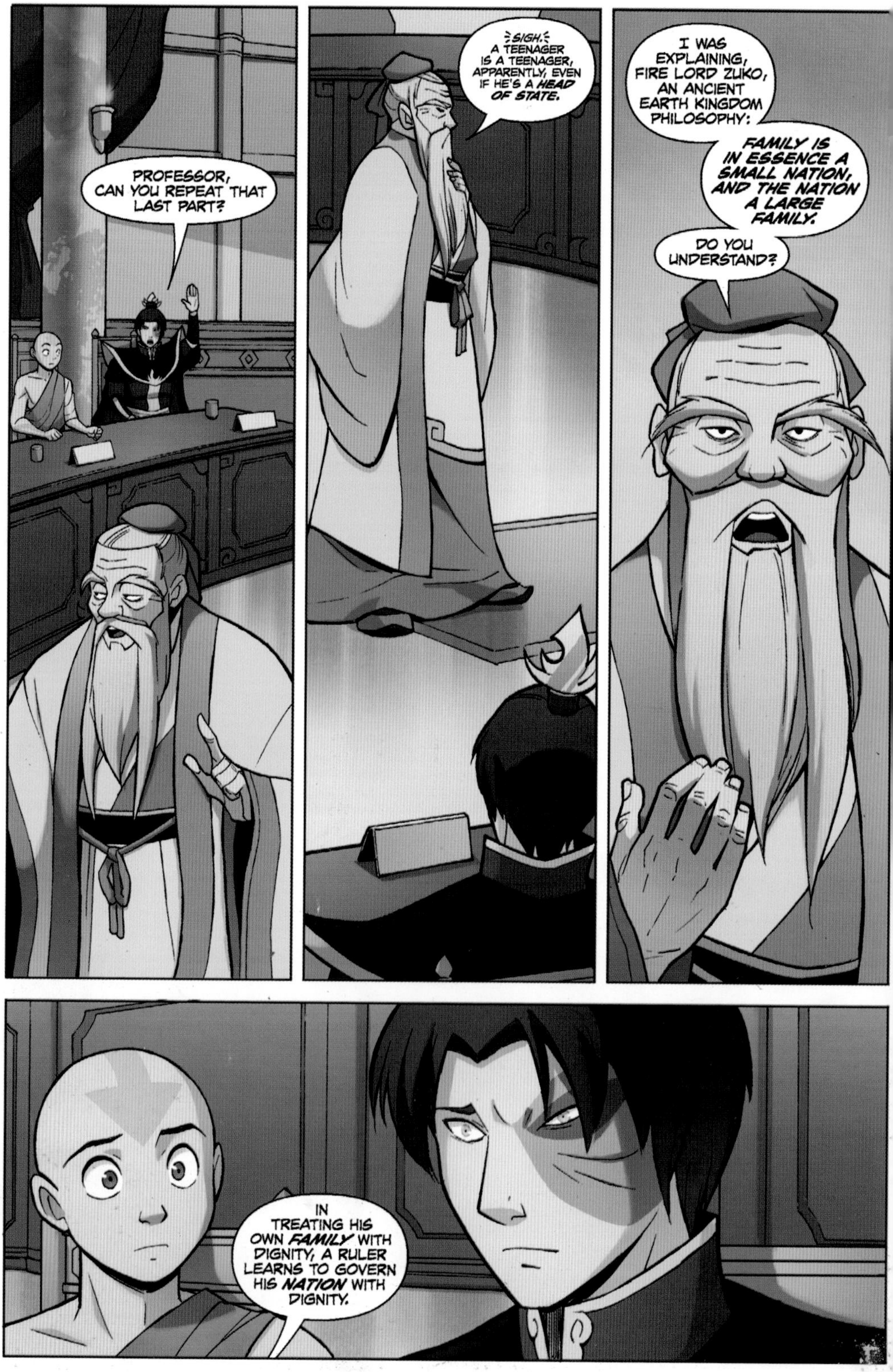
PROFESSOR, CAN YOU REPEAT THAT LAST PART?
SIGH. A TEENAGER IS A TEENAGER, APPARENTLY, EVEN IF HE'S A HEAD OF STATE.
I WAS EXPLAINING, FIRE LORD ZUKO, AN ANCIENT EARTH KINGDOM PHILOSOPHY:
FAMILY IS IN ESSENCE A SMALL NATION, AND THE NATION A LARGE FAMILY.
DO YOU UNDERSTAND?
IN TREATING HIS OWN FAMILY WITH DIGNITY, A RULER LEARNS TO GOVERN HIS NATION WITH DIGNITY.

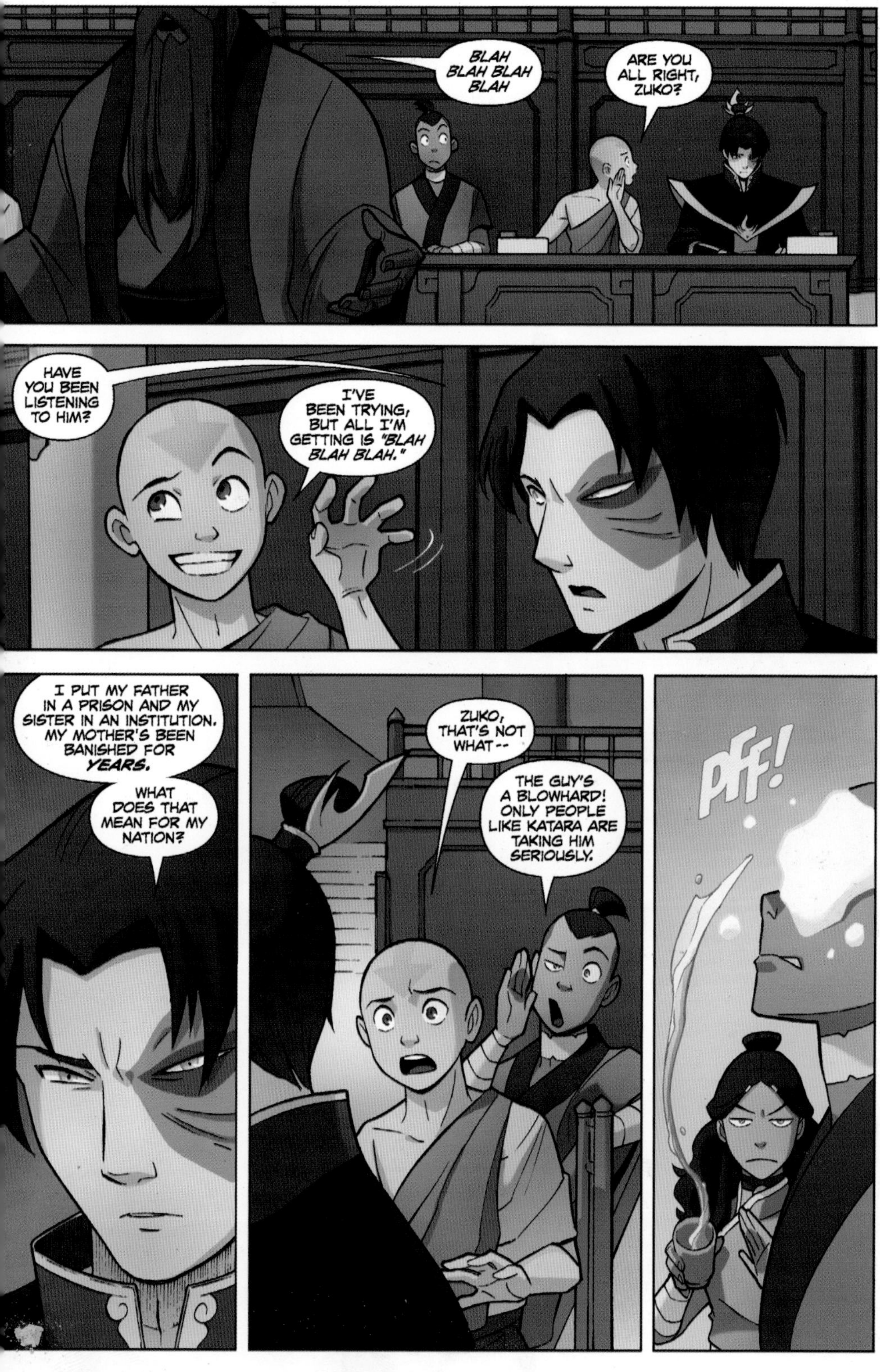
BLAH BLAH BLAH BLAH
ARE YOU ALL RIGHT, ZUKO?
HAVE YOU BEEN LISTENING TO HIM?
I'VE BEEN TRYING, BUT ALL I'M GETTING IS "BLAH BLAH BLAH."
I PUT MY FATHER IN A PRISON AND MY SISTER IN AN INSTITUTION. MY MOTHER'S BEEN BANISHED FOR YEARS.
WHAT DOES THAT MEAN FOR MY NATION?
ZUKO, THAT'S NOT WHAT--
THE GUY'S A BLOWHARD! ONLY PEOPLE LIKE KATARA ARE TAKING HIM SERIOUSLY.
PFF!

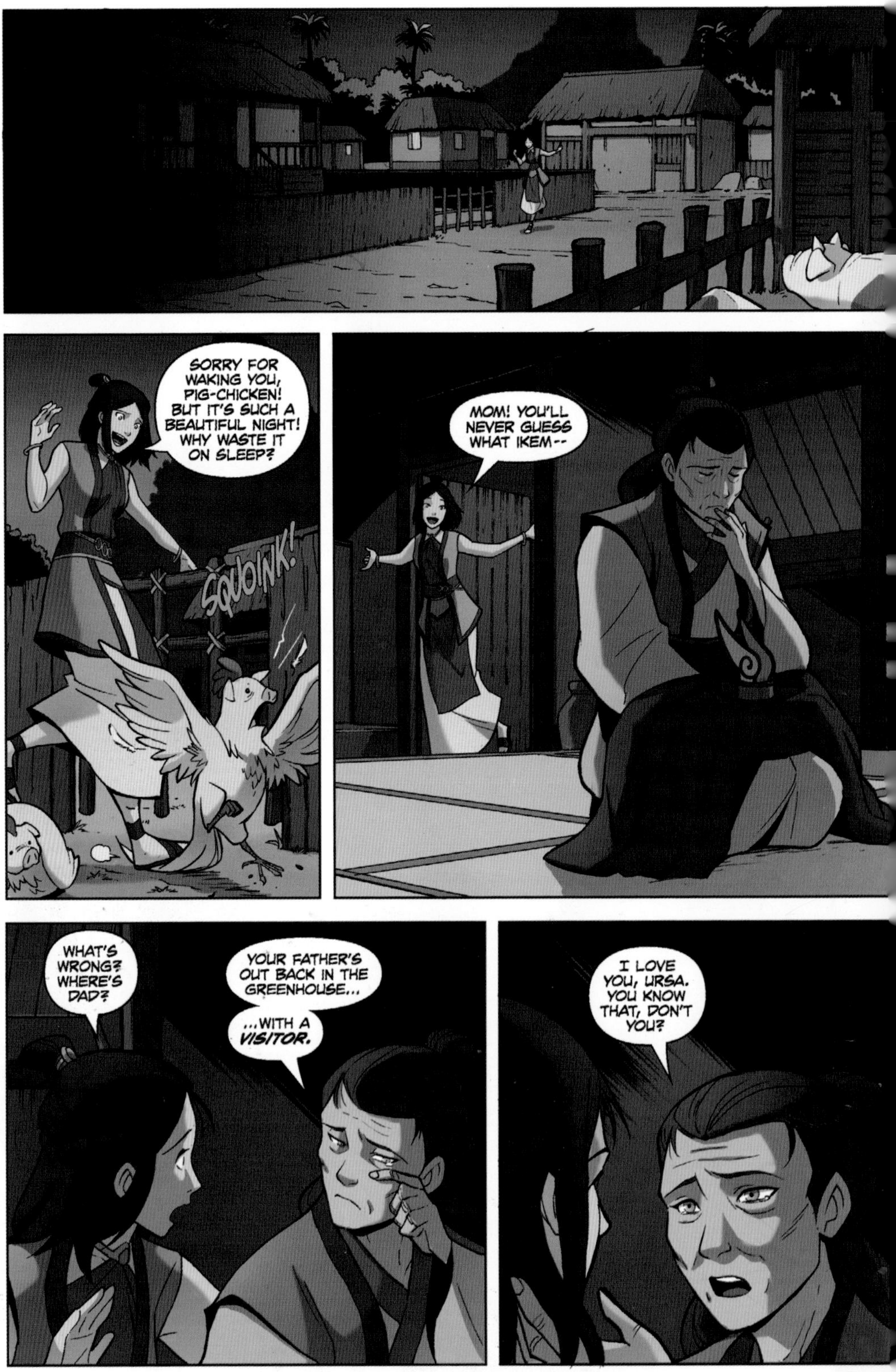
SORRY FOR WAKING YOU, PIG-CHICKEN! BUT IT'S SUCH A BEAUTIFUL NIGHT! WHY WASTE IT ON SLEEP?
SQUOINK!
MOM! YOU'LL NEVER GUESS WHAT IKEM--
WHAT'S WRONG? WHERE'S DAD?
YOUR FATHER'S OUT BACK IN THE GREENHOUSE...
...WITH A VISITOR.
I LOVE YOU, URSA. YOU KNOW THAT, DON'T YOU?

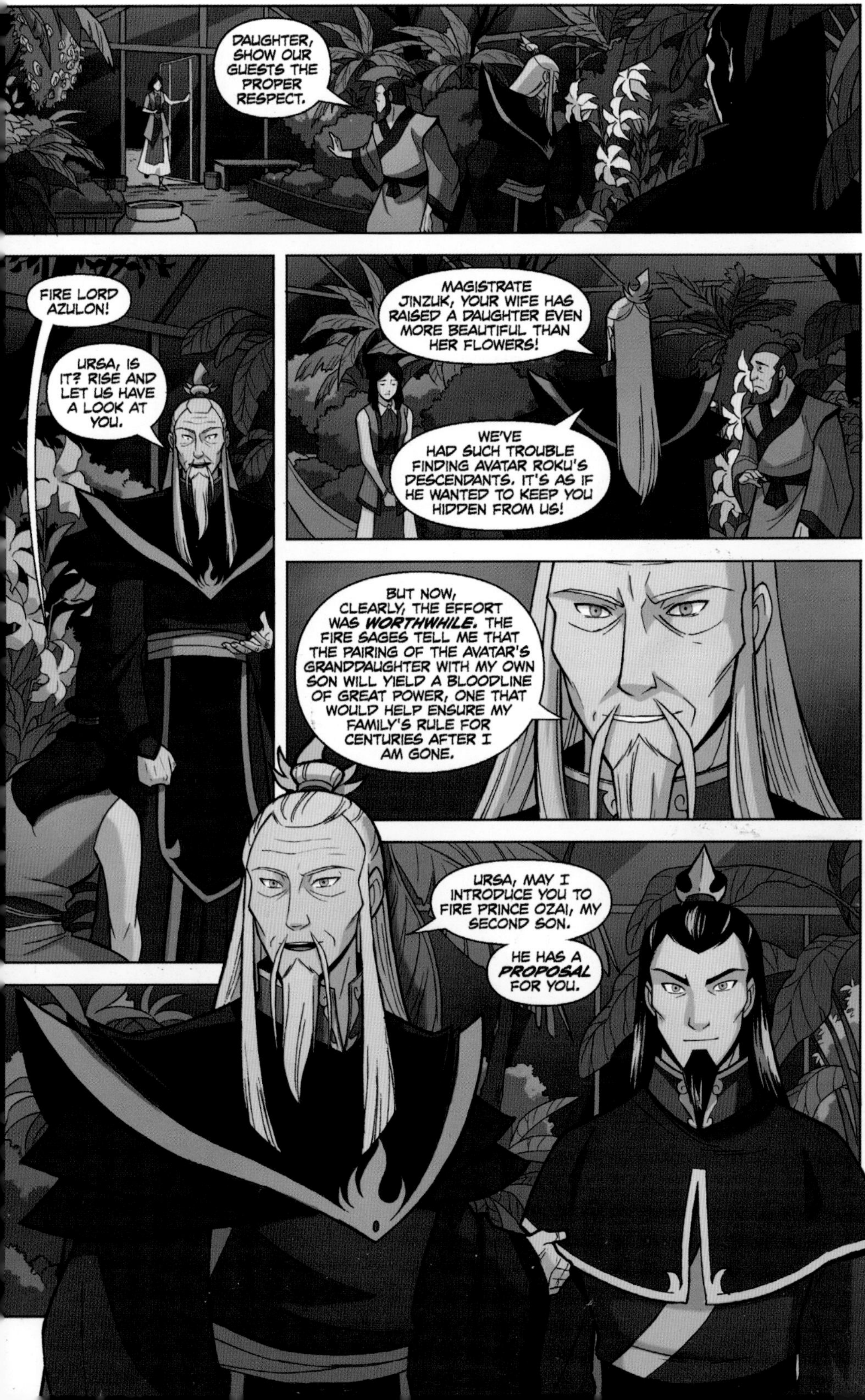
DAUGHTER, SHOW OUR GUESTS THE PROPER RESPECT.
FIRE LORD AZULON!
URSA, IS IT? RISE AND LET US HAVE A LOOK AT YOU.
MAGISTRATE JINZUK, YOUR WIFE HAS RAISED A DAUGHTER EVEN MORE BEAUTIFUL THAN HER FLOWERS!
WE'VE HAD SUCH TROUBLE FINDING AVATAR ROKU'S DESCENDANTS. IT'S AS IF HE WANTED TO KEEP YOU HIDDEN FROM US!
BUT NOW, CLEARLY, THE EFFORT WAS WORTHWHILE. THE FIRE SAGES TELL ME THAT THE PAIRING OF THE AVATAR'S GRANDDAUGHTER WITH MY OWN SON WILL YIELD A BLOODLINE OF GREAT POWER, ONE THAT WOULD HELP ENSURE MY FAMILY'S RULE FOR CENTURIES AFTER I AM GONE.
URSA, MAY I INTRODUCE YOU TO FIRE PRINCE OZAI, MY SECOND SON.
HE HAS A PROPOSAL FOR YOU.

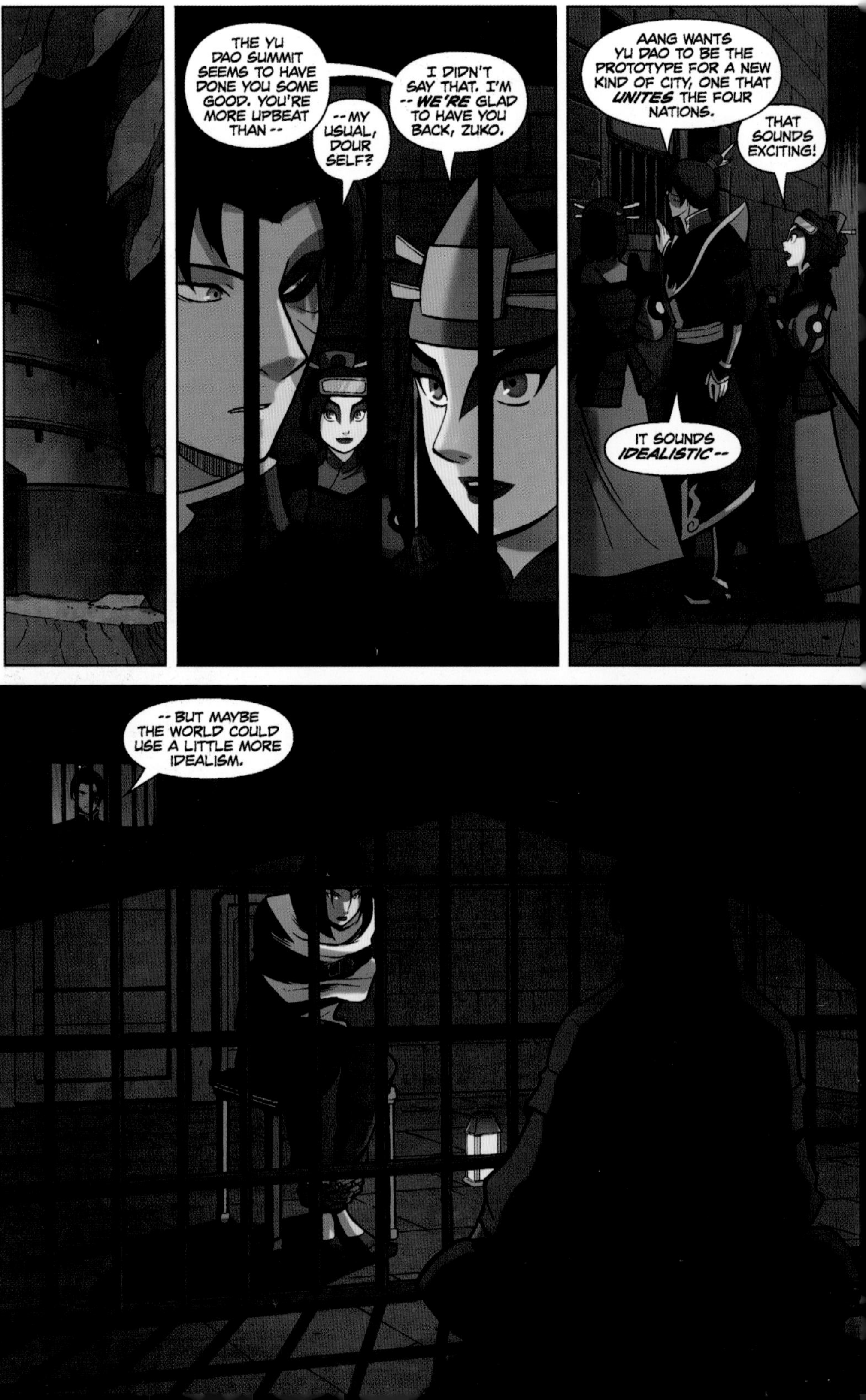
THE YU DAO SUMMIT SEEMS TO HAVE DONE YOU SOME GOOD. YOU'RE MORE UPBEAT THAN --
-- MY USUAL, DOUR SELF?
I DIDN'T SAY THAT. I'M -- WE'RE GLAD TO HAVE YOU BACK, ZUKO.
AANG WANTS YU DAO TO BE THE PROTOTYPE FOR A NEW KIND OF CITY, ONE THAT UNITES THE FOUR NATIONS.
THAT SOUNDS EXCITING!
IT SOUNDS IDEALISTIC --
-- BUT MAYBE THE WORLD COULD USE A LITTLE MORE IDEALISM.

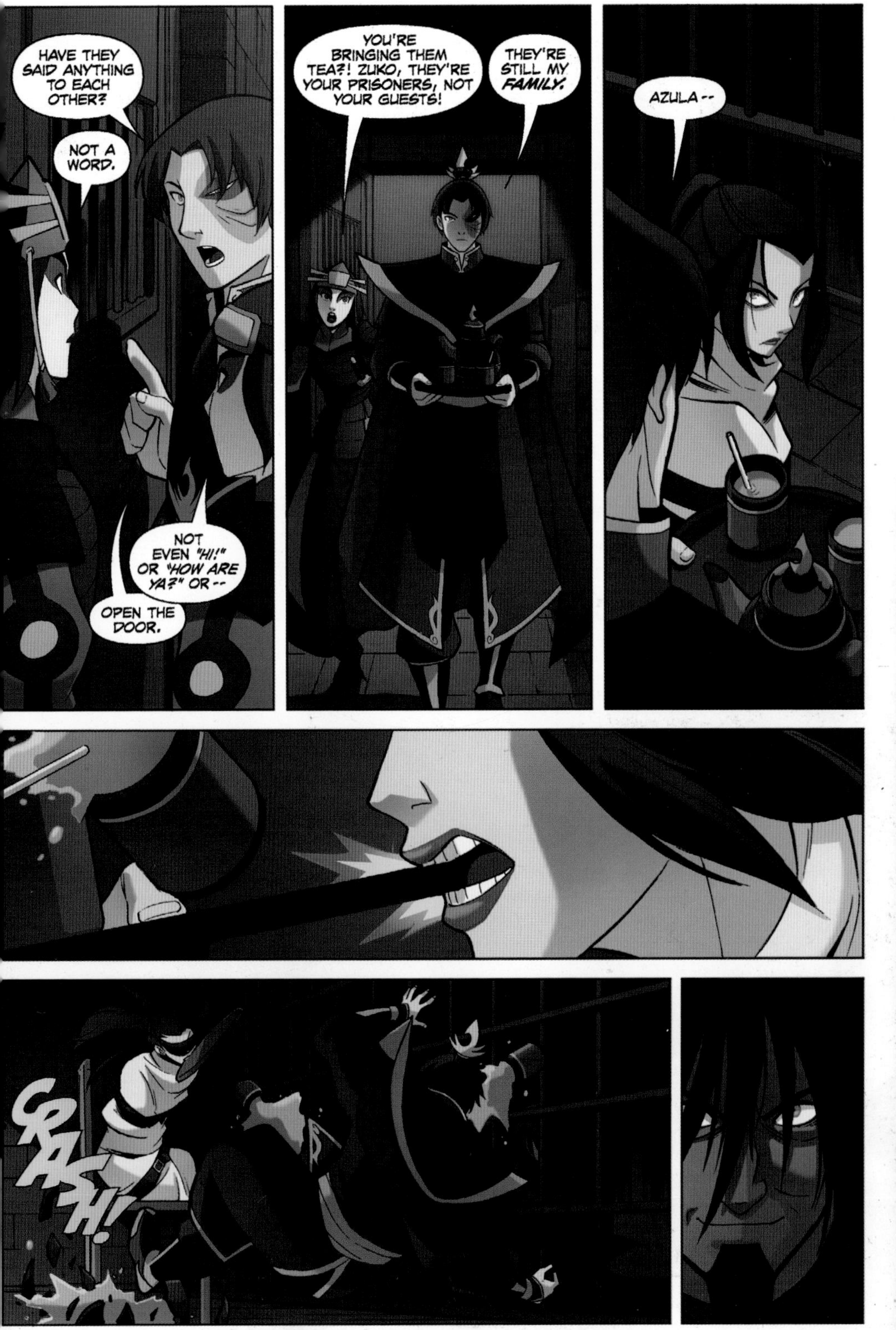
HAVE THEY SAID ANYTHING TO EACH OTHER?
NOT A WORD.
NOT EVEN "HI!" OR "HOW ARE YA?" OR --
OPEN THE DOOR.
YOU'RE BRINGING THEM TEA?! ZUKO, THEY'RE YOUR PRISONERS, NOT YOUR GUESTS!
THEY'RE STILL MY FAMILY.
AZULA --
CRASH!

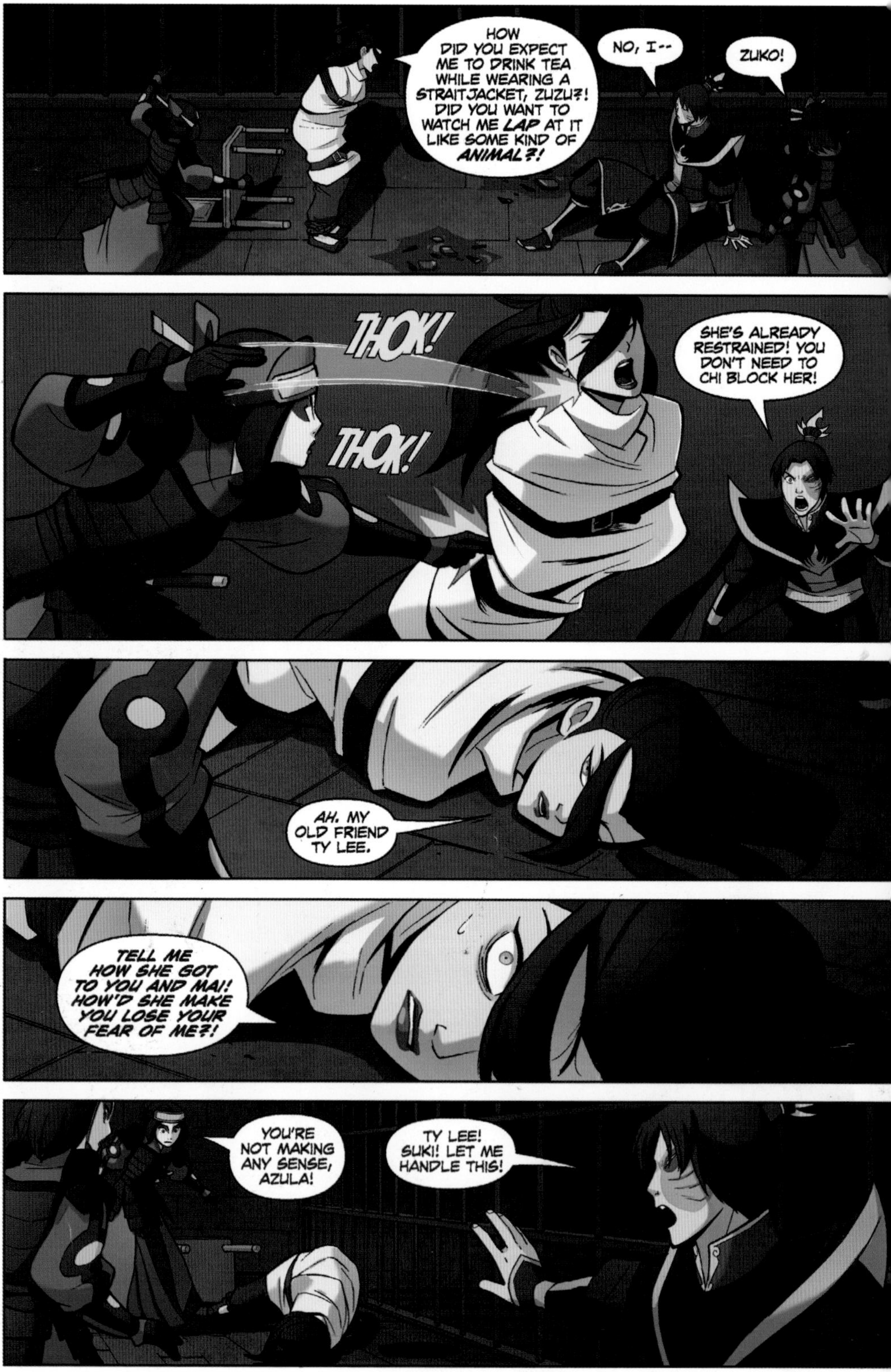
HOW DID YOU EXPECT ME TO DRINK TEA WHILE WEARING A STRAITJACKET, ZUZU?! DID YOU WANT TO WATCH ME *LAP* AT IT LIKE SOME KIND OF *ANIMAL?!*
NO, I--
ZUKO!
THOK!
THOK!
SHE'S ALREADY RESTRAINED! YOU DON'T NEED TO CHI BLOCK HER!
AH. MY OLD FRIEND TY LEE.
TELL ME HOW SHE GOT TO YOU AND MAI! HOW'D SHE MAKE YOU LOSE YOUR FEAR OF ME?!
YOU'RE NOT MAKING ANY SENSE, AZULA!
TY LEE! SUKI! LET ME HANDLE THIS!

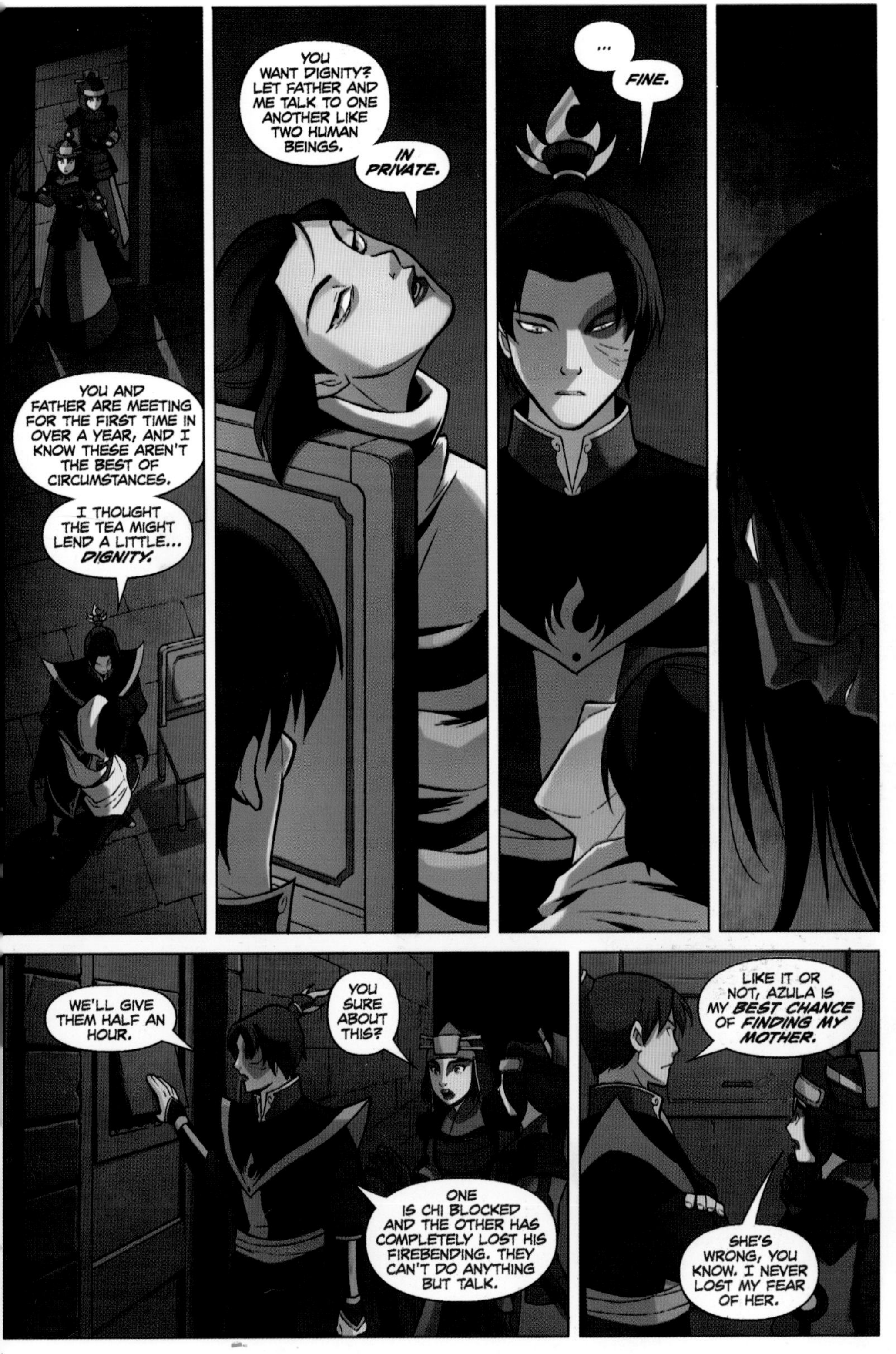
YOU AND FATHER ARE MEETING FOR THE FIRST TIME IN OVER A YEAR, AND I KNOW THESE AREN'T THE BEST OF CIRCUMSTANCES.
I THOUGHT THE TEA MIGHT LEND A LITTLE... DIGNITY.
YOU WANT DIGNITY? LET FATHER AND ME TALK TO ONE ANOTHER LIKE TWO HUMAN BEINGS.
IN PRIVATE.
...
FINE.
WE'LL GIVE THEM HALF AN HOUR.
YOU SURE ABOUT THIS?
ONE IS CHI BLOCKED AND THE OTHER HAS COMPLETELY LOST HIS FIREBENDING. THEY CAN'T DO ANYTHING BUT TALK.
LIKE IT OR NOT, AZULA IS MY BEST CHANCE OF FINDING MY MOTHER.
SHE'S WRONG, YOU KNOW. I NEVER LOST MY FEAR OF HER.

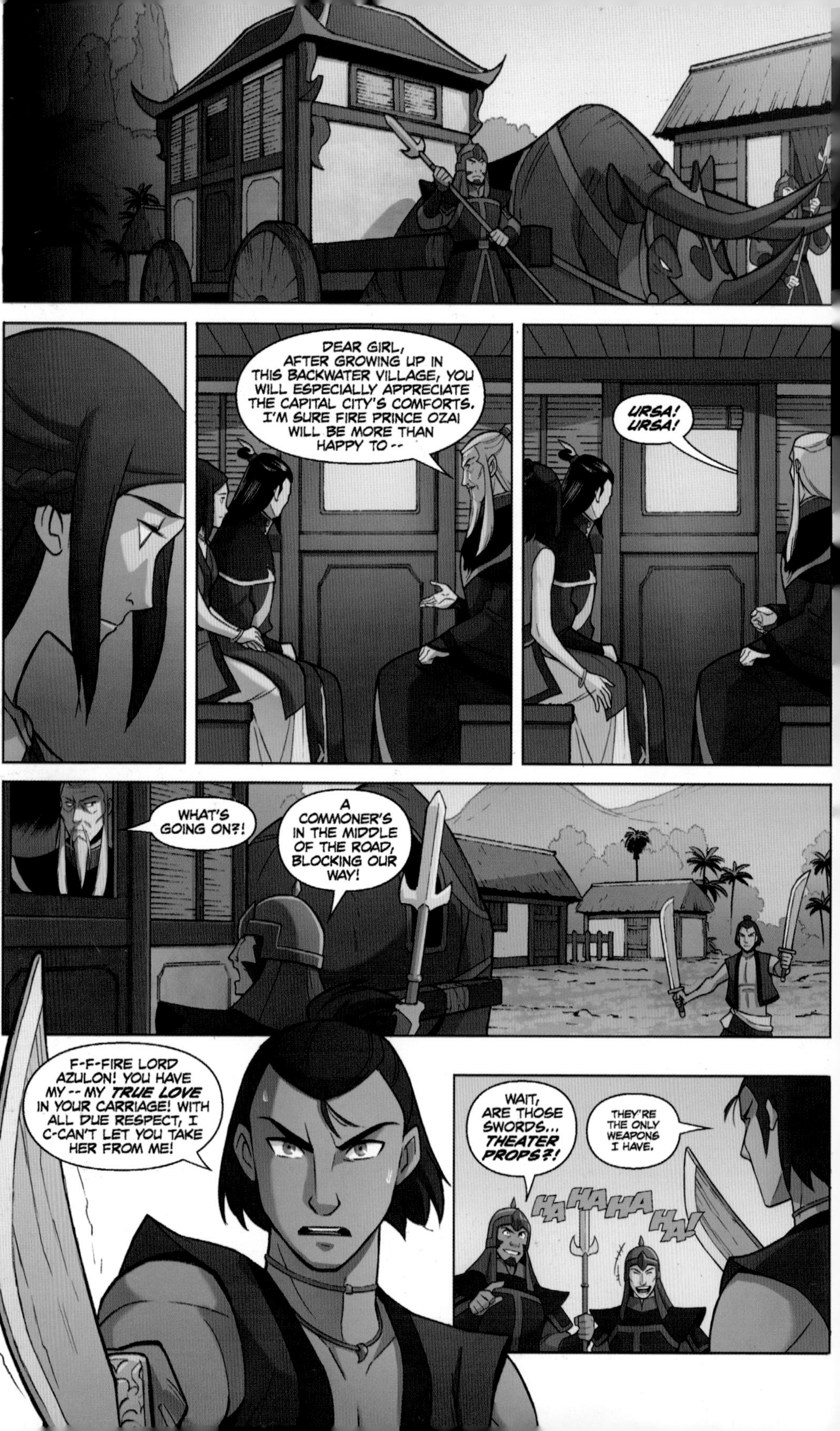

DEAR GIRL, AFTER GROWING UP IN THIS BACKWATER VILLAGE, YOU WILL ESPECIALLY APPRECIATE THE CAPITAL CITY'S COMFORTS. I'M SURE FIRE PRINCE OZAI WILL BE MORE THAN HAPPY TO --
URSA! URSA!
WHAT'S GOING ON?!
A COMMONER'S IN THE MIDDLE OF THE ROAD, BLOCKING OUR WAY!
F-F-FIRE LORD AZULON! YOU HAVE MY -- MY TRUE LOVE IN YOUR CARRIAGE! WITH ALL DUE RESPECT, I C-CAN'T LET YOU TAKE HER FROM ME!
WAIT, ARE THOSE SWORDS... THEATER PROPS?!
THEY'RE THE ONLY WEAPONS I HAVE.
HA HA HA HA HA!

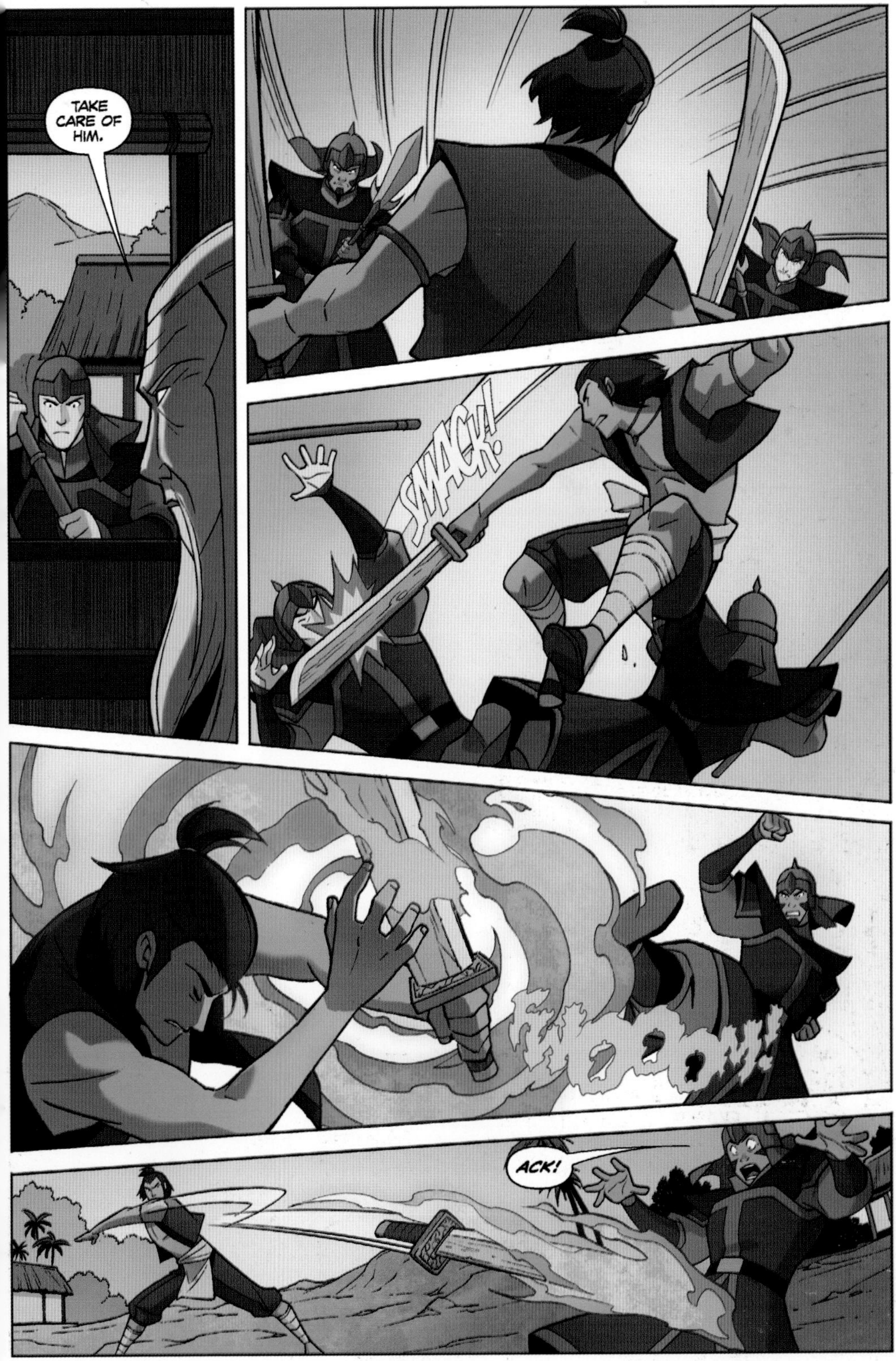
TAKE CARE OF HIM.
SMACK!
FWOOM!
ACK!

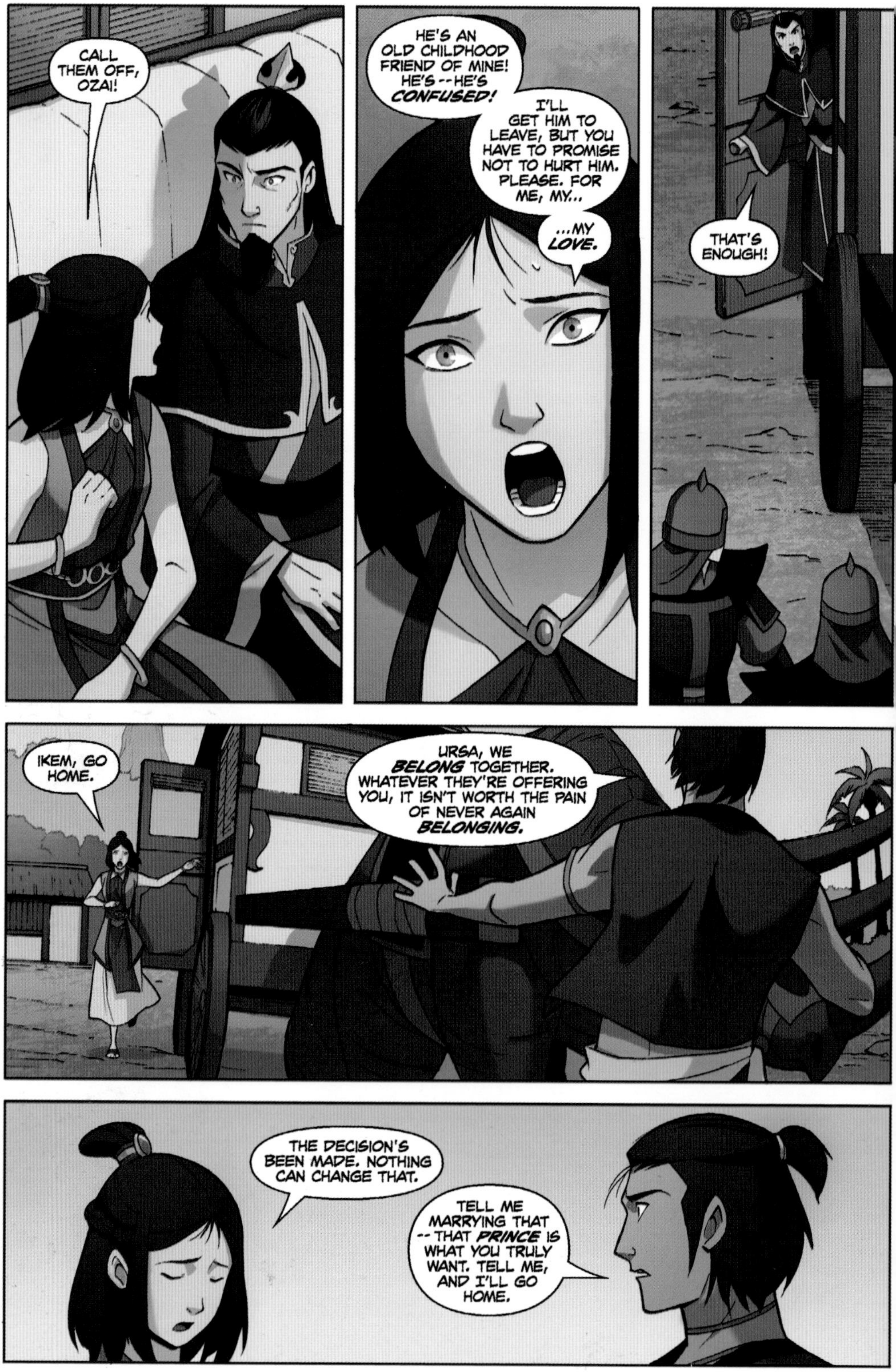
CALL THEM OFF, OZAI!
HE'S AN OLD CHILDHOOD FRIEND OF MINE! HE'S--HE'S CONFUSED!
I'LL GET HIM TO LEAVE, BUT YOU HAVE TO PROMISE NOT TO HURT HIM. PLEASE. FOR ME, MY...
...MY LOVE.
THAT'S ENOUGH!
IKEM, GO HOME.
URSA, WE BELONG TOGETHER. WHATEVER THEY'RE OFFERING YOU, IT ISN'T WORTH THE PAIN OF NEVER AGAIN BELONGING.
THE DECISION'S BEEN MADE. NOTHING CAN CHANGE THAT.
TELL ME MARRYING THAT --THAT PRINCE IS WHAT YOU TRULY WANT. TELL ME, AND I'LL GO HOME.

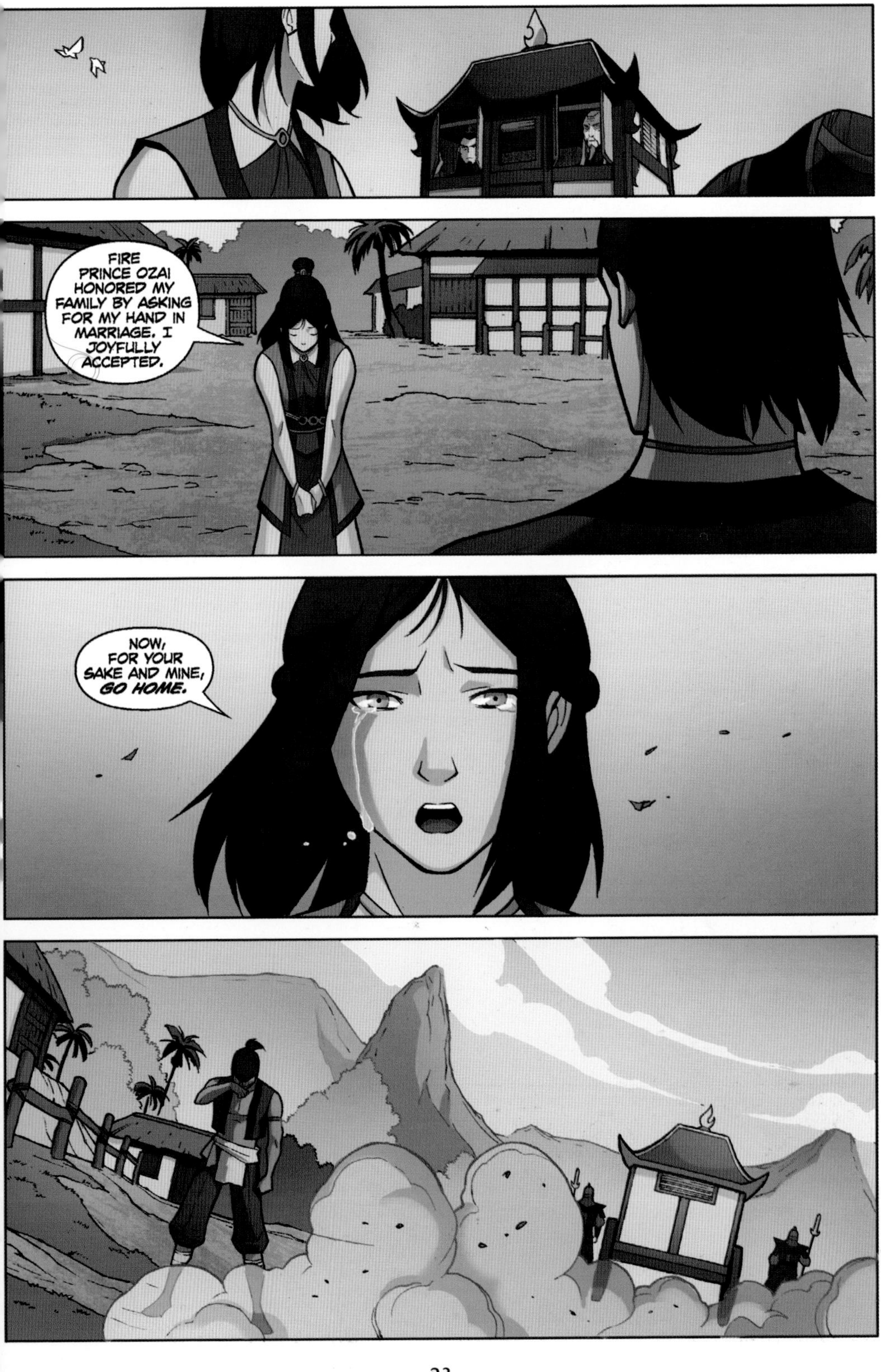
FIRE PRINCE OZAI HONORED MY FAMILY BY ASKING FOR MY HAND IN MARRIAGE. I JOYFULLY ACCEPTED.
NOW, FOR YOUR SAKE AND MINE, *GO HOME.*

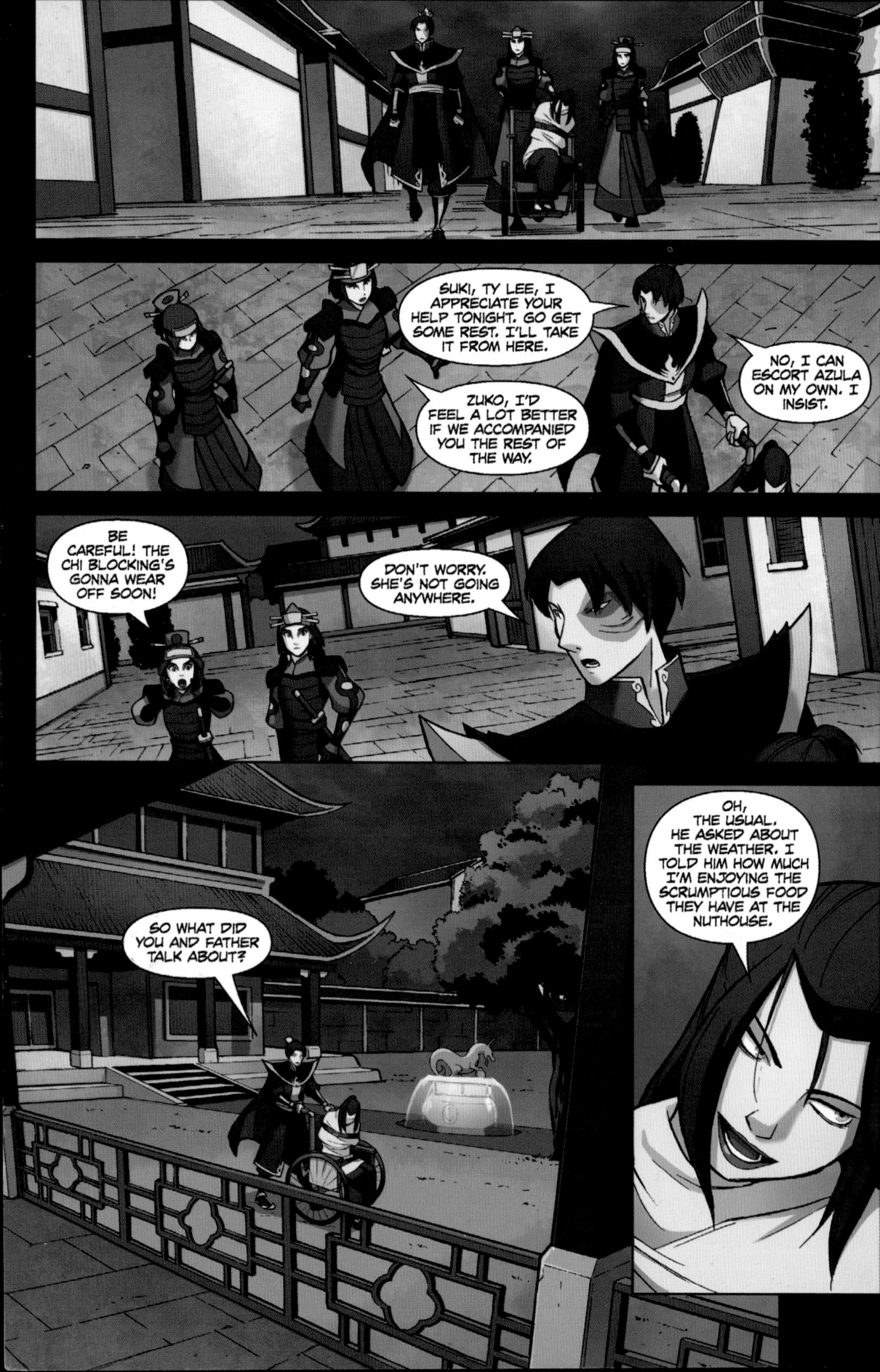
SUKI, TY LEE, I APPRECIATE YOUR HELP TONIGHT. GO GET SOME REST. I'LL TAKE IT FROM HERE.
ZUKO, I'D FEEL A LOT BETTER IF WE ACCOMPANIED YOU THE REST OF THE WAY.
NO, I CAN ESCORT AZULA ON MY OWN. I INSIST.
BE CAREFUL! THE CHI BLOCKING'S GONNA WEAR OFF SOON!
DON'T WORRY. SHE'S NOT GOING ANYWHERE.
SO WHAT DID YOU AND FATHER TALK ABOUT?
OH, THE USUAL. HE ASKED ABOUT THE WEATHER. I TOLD HIM HOW MUCH I'M ENJOYING THE SCRUMPTIOUS FOOD THEY HAVE AT THE NUTHOUSE.

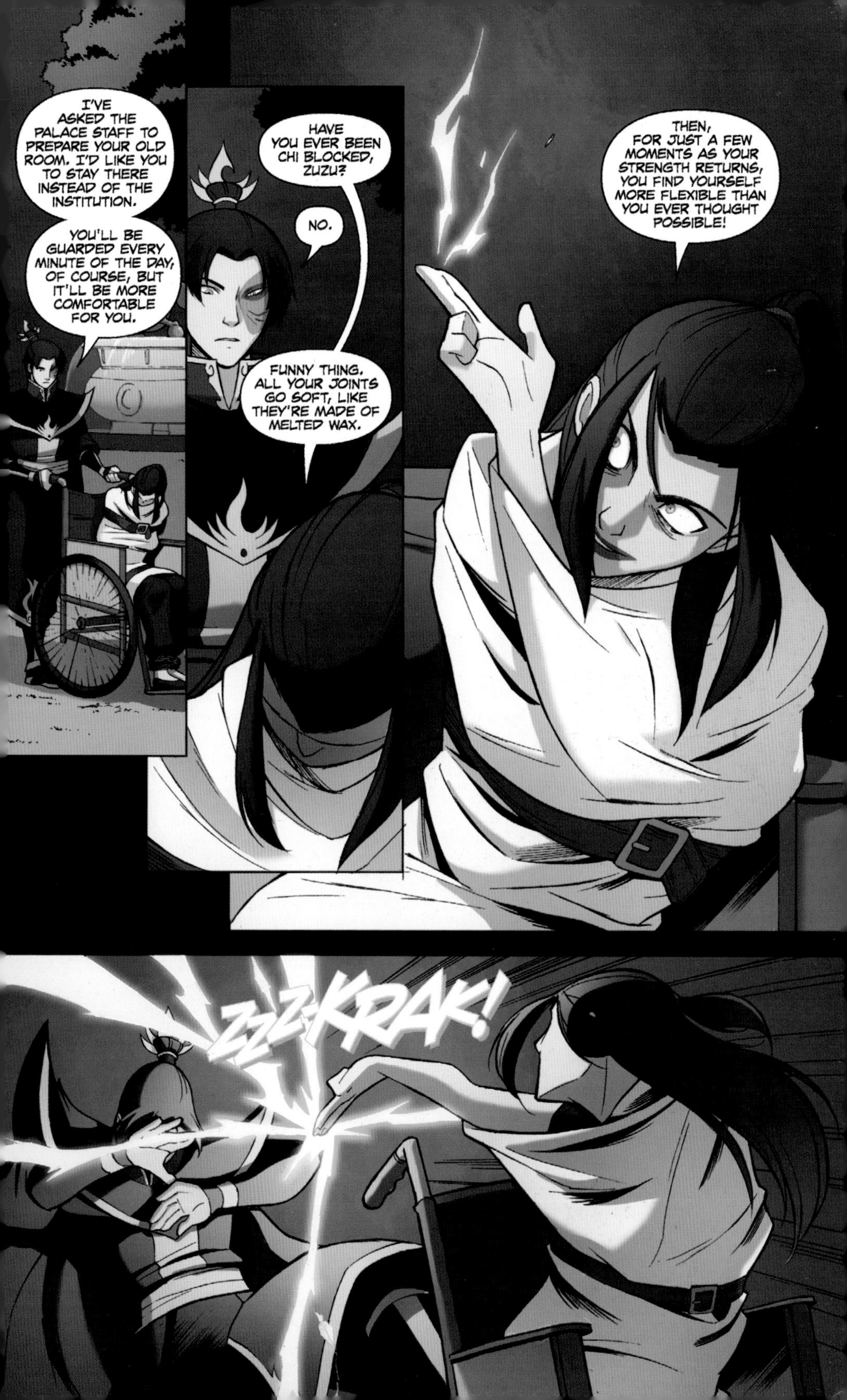
I'VE ASKED THE PALACE STAFF TO PREPARE YOUR OLD ROOM. I'D LIKE YOU TO STAY THERE INSTEAD OF THE INSTITUTION.
YOU'LL BE GUARDED EVERY MINUTE OF THE DAY, OF COURSE, BUT IT'LL BE MORE COMFORTABLE FOR YOU.
HAVE YOU EVER BEEN CHI BLOCKED, ZUZU?
NO.
FUNNY THING. ALL YOUR JOINTS GO SOFT, LIKE THEY'RE MADE OF MELTED WAX.
THEN, FOR JUST A FEW MOMENTS AS YOUR STRENGTH RETURNS, YOU FIND YOURSELF MORE FLEXIBLE THAN YOU EVER THOUGHT POSSIBLE!
ZZZ-KRAK!

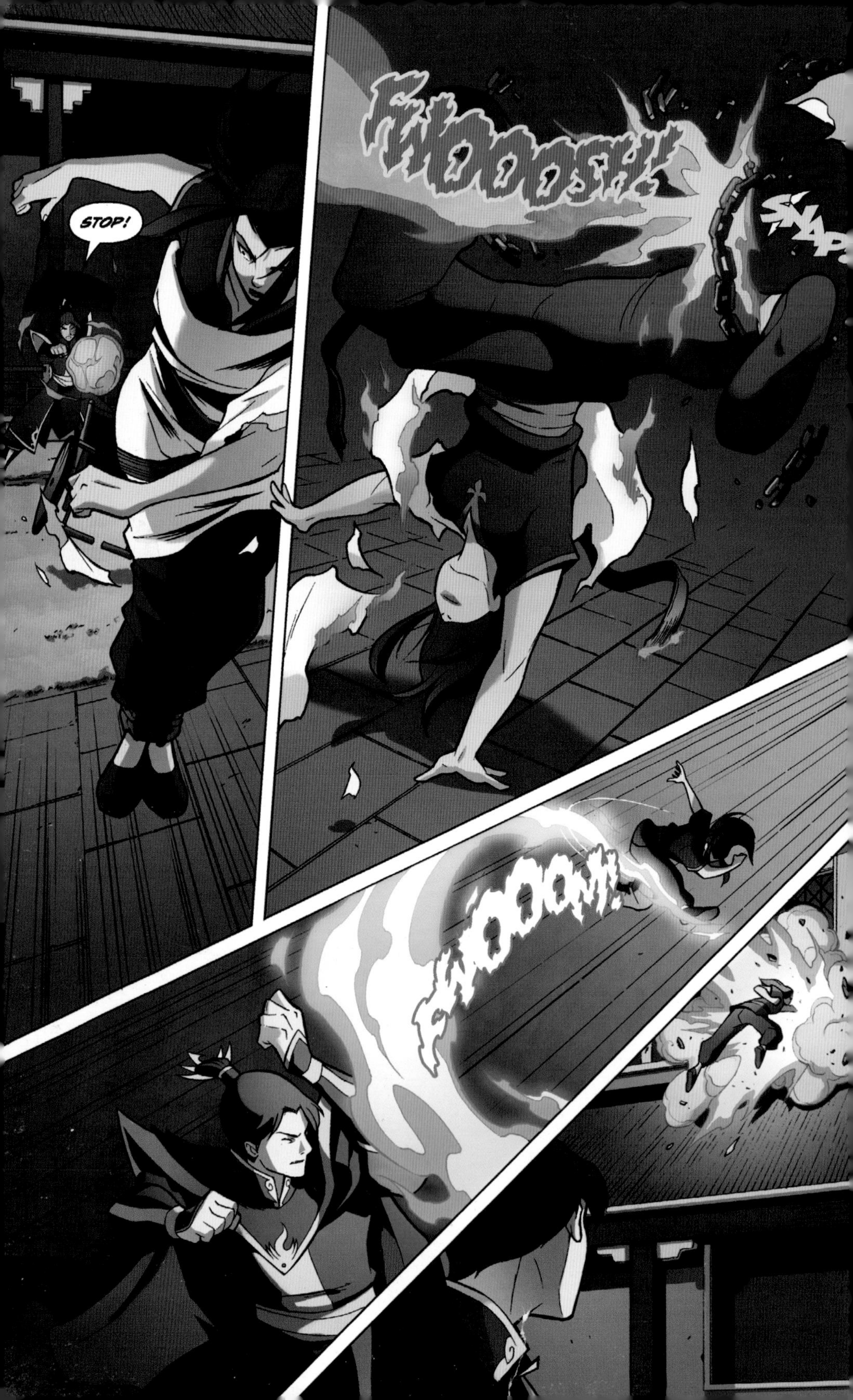
STOP!
FWOOOSH!
SNAP!
FWOOOM!

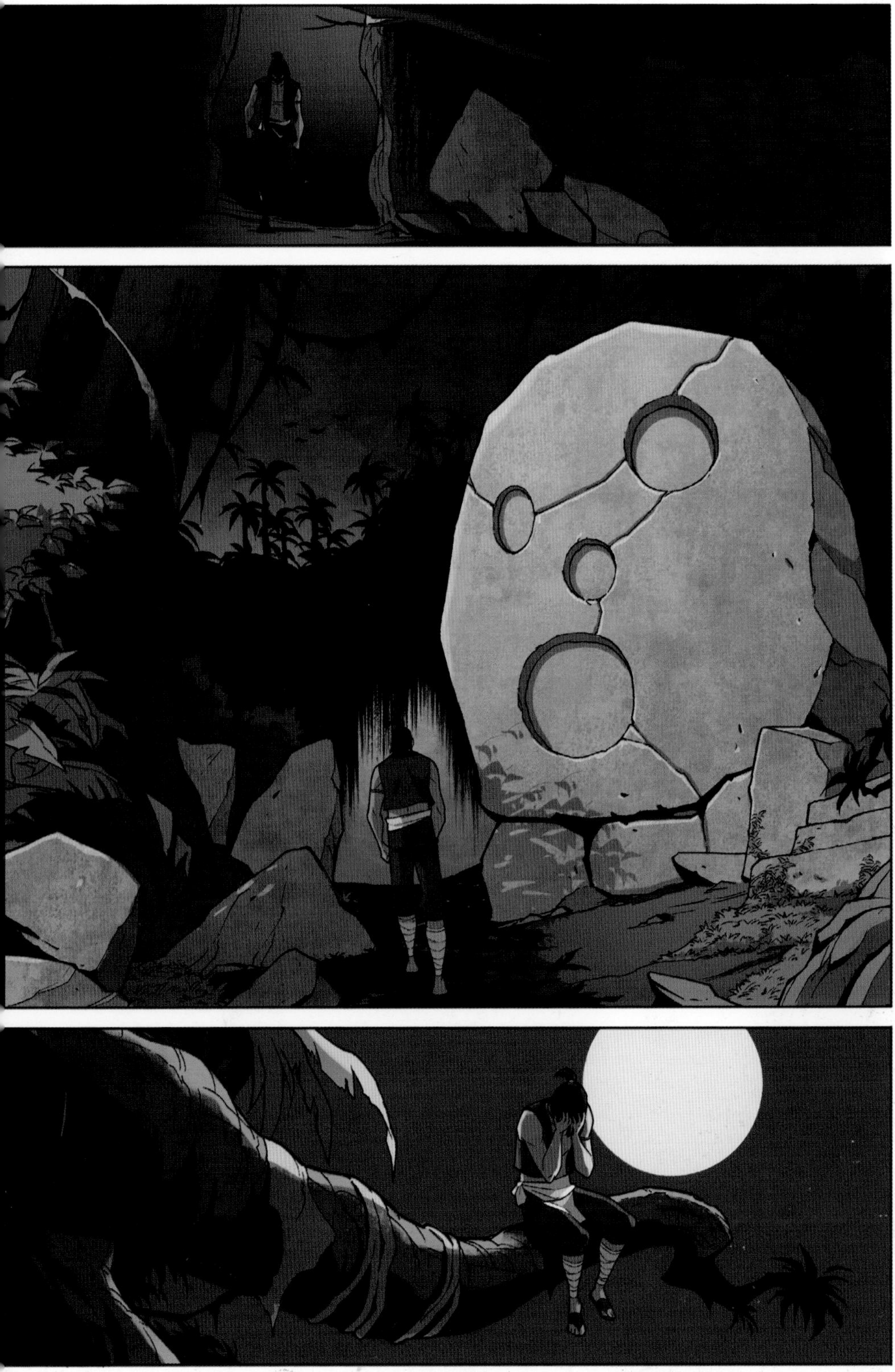

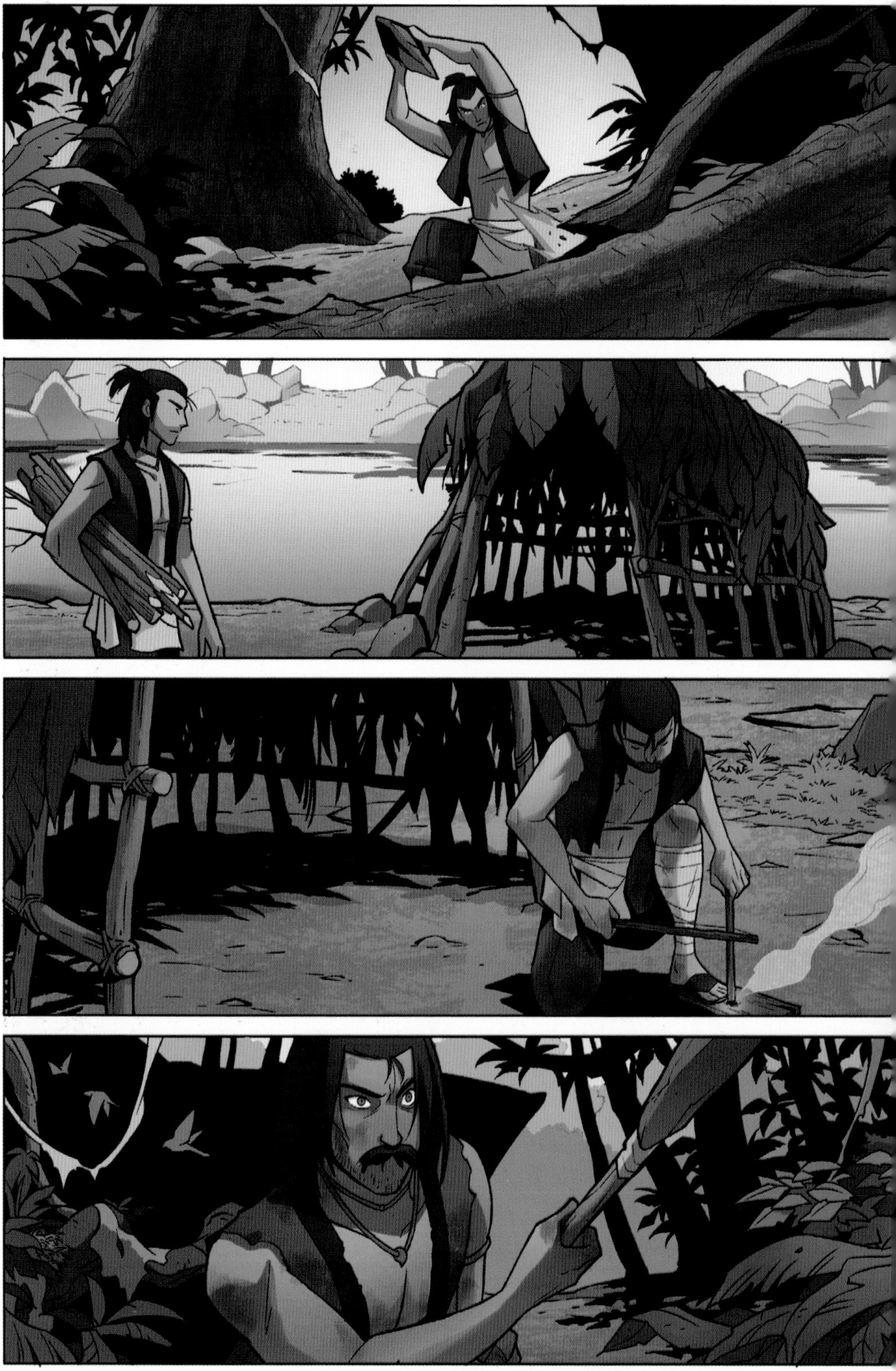

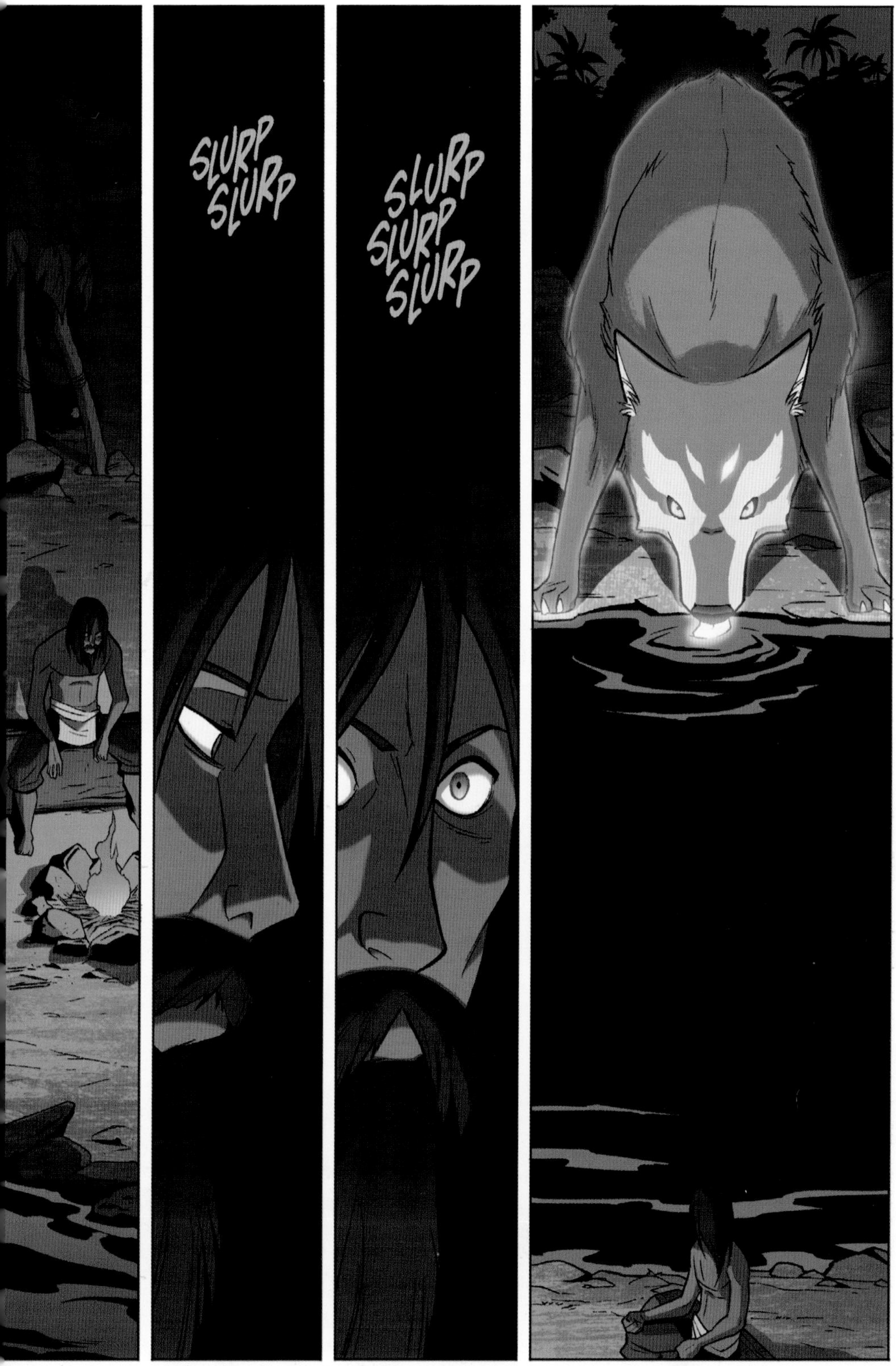
SLURP
SLURP
SLURP
SLURP
SLURP

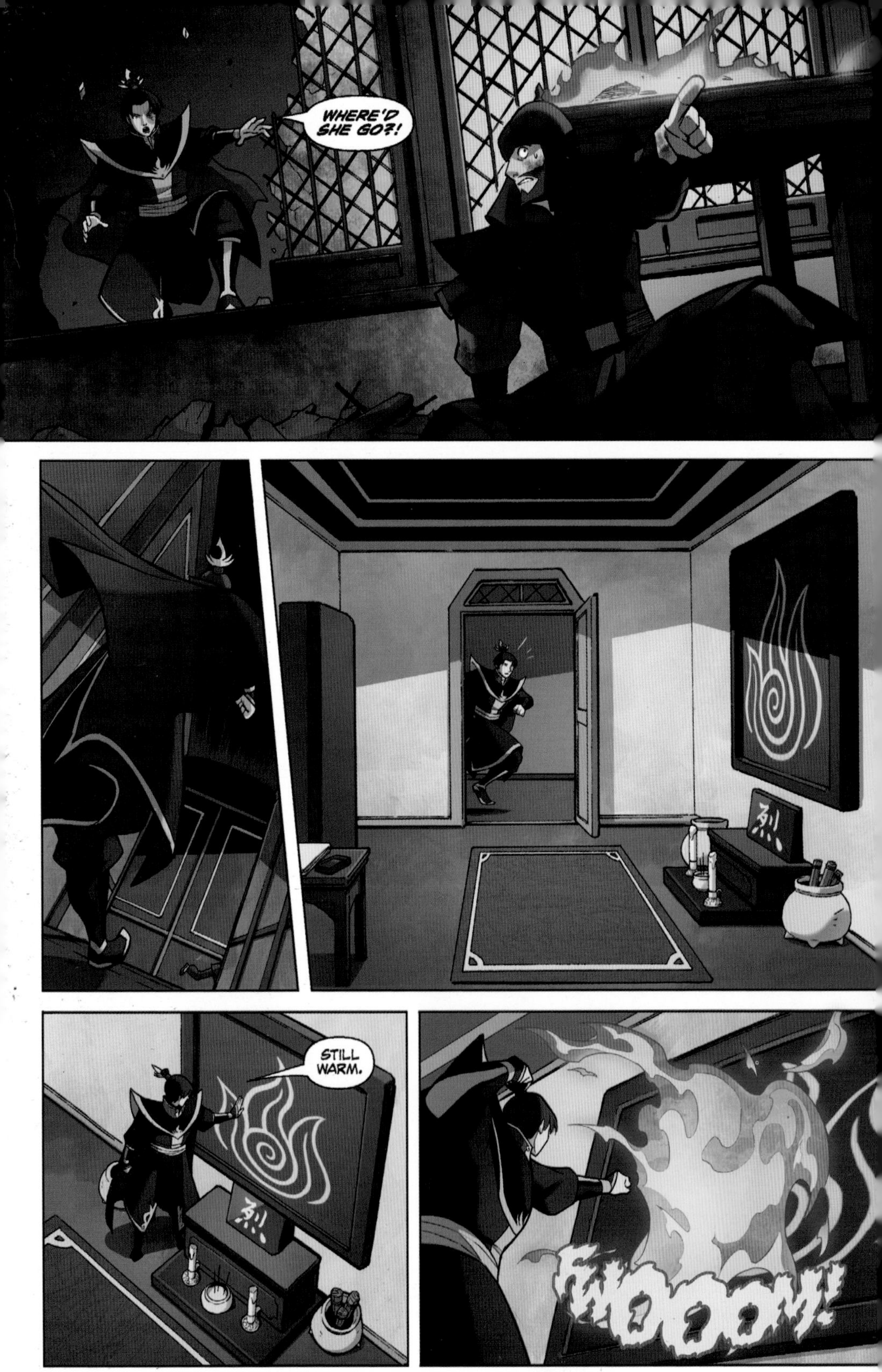
WHERE'D SHE GO?!
STILL WARM.
FWOOOM!

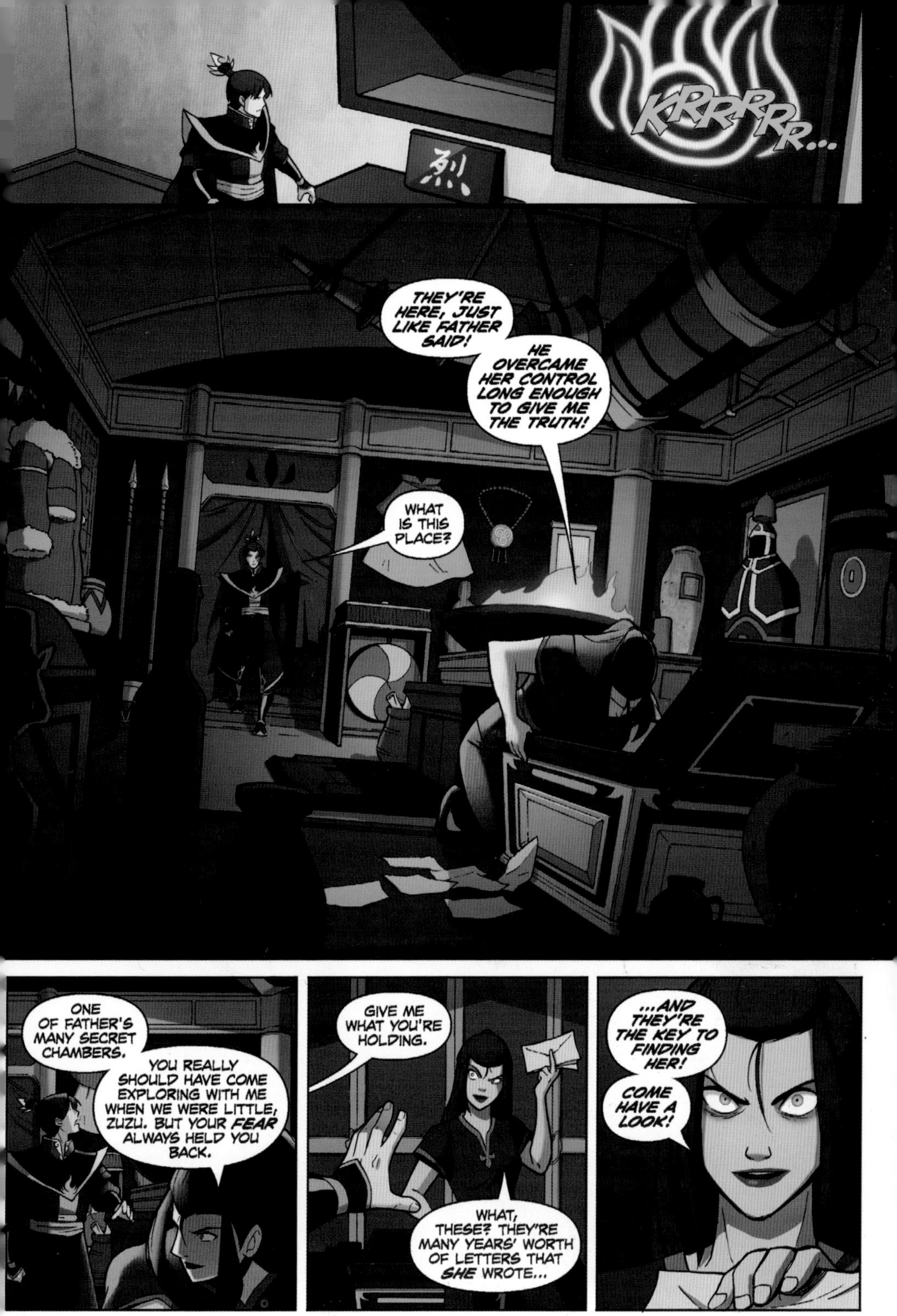
KRRRRR...
THEY'RE HERE, JUST LIKE FATHER SAID!
HE OVERCAME HER CONTROL LONG ENOUGH TO GIVE ME THE TRUTH!
WHAT IS THIS PLACE?
ONE OF FATHER'S MANY SECRET CHAMBERS.
YOU REALLY SHOULD HAVE COME EXPLORING WITH ME WHEN WE WERE LITTLE, ZUZU. BUT YOUR *FEAR* ALWAYS HELD YOU BACK.
GIVE ME WHAT YOU'RE HOLDING.
WHAT, THESE? THEY'RE MANY YEARS' WORTH OF LETTERS THAT *SHE* WROTE...
...AND THEY'RE THE KEY TO FINDING HER!
COME HAVE A LOOK!

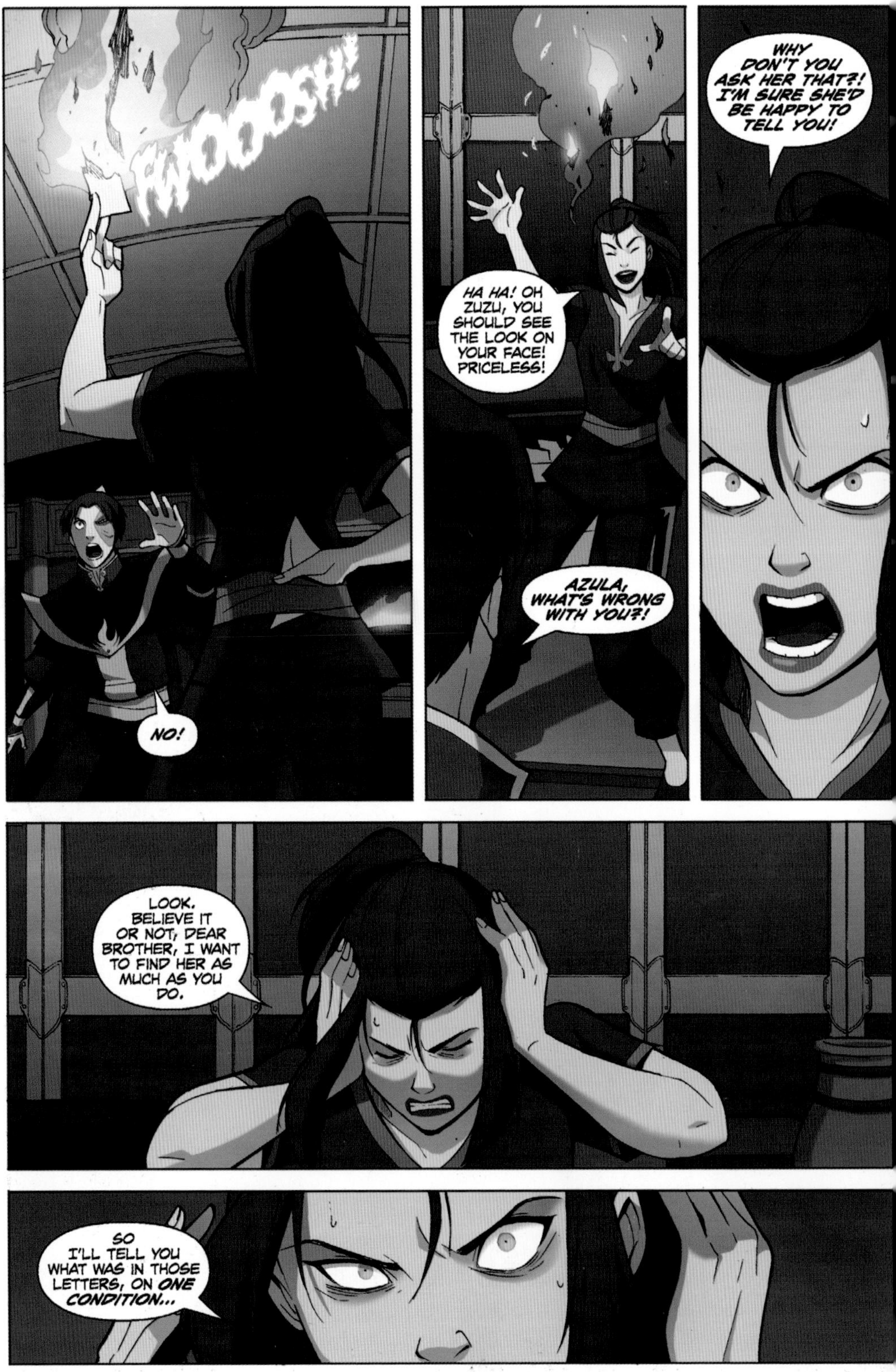
FWOOOSH!
NO!
HA HA! OH ZUZU, YOU SHOULD SEE THE LOOK ON YOUR FACE! PRICELESS!
AZULA, WHAT'S WRONG WITH YOU?!
WHY DON'T YOU ASK HER THAT?! I'M SURE SHE'D BE HAPPY TO TELL YOU!
LOOK. BELIEVE IT OR NOT, DEAR BROTHER, I WANT TO FIND HER AS MUCH AS YOU DO.
SO I'LL TELL YOU WHAT WAS IN THOSE LETTERS, ON ONE CONDITION...

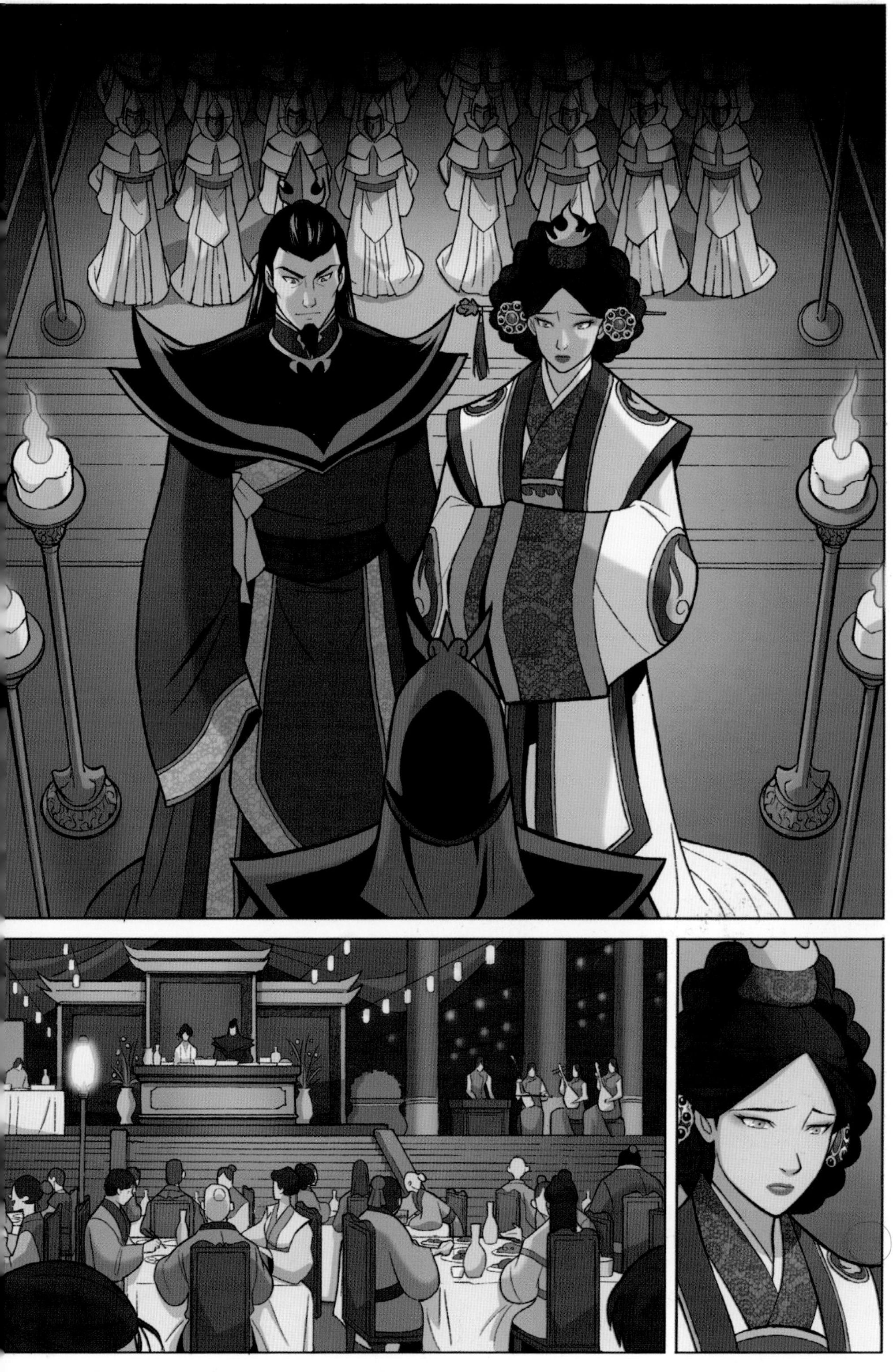

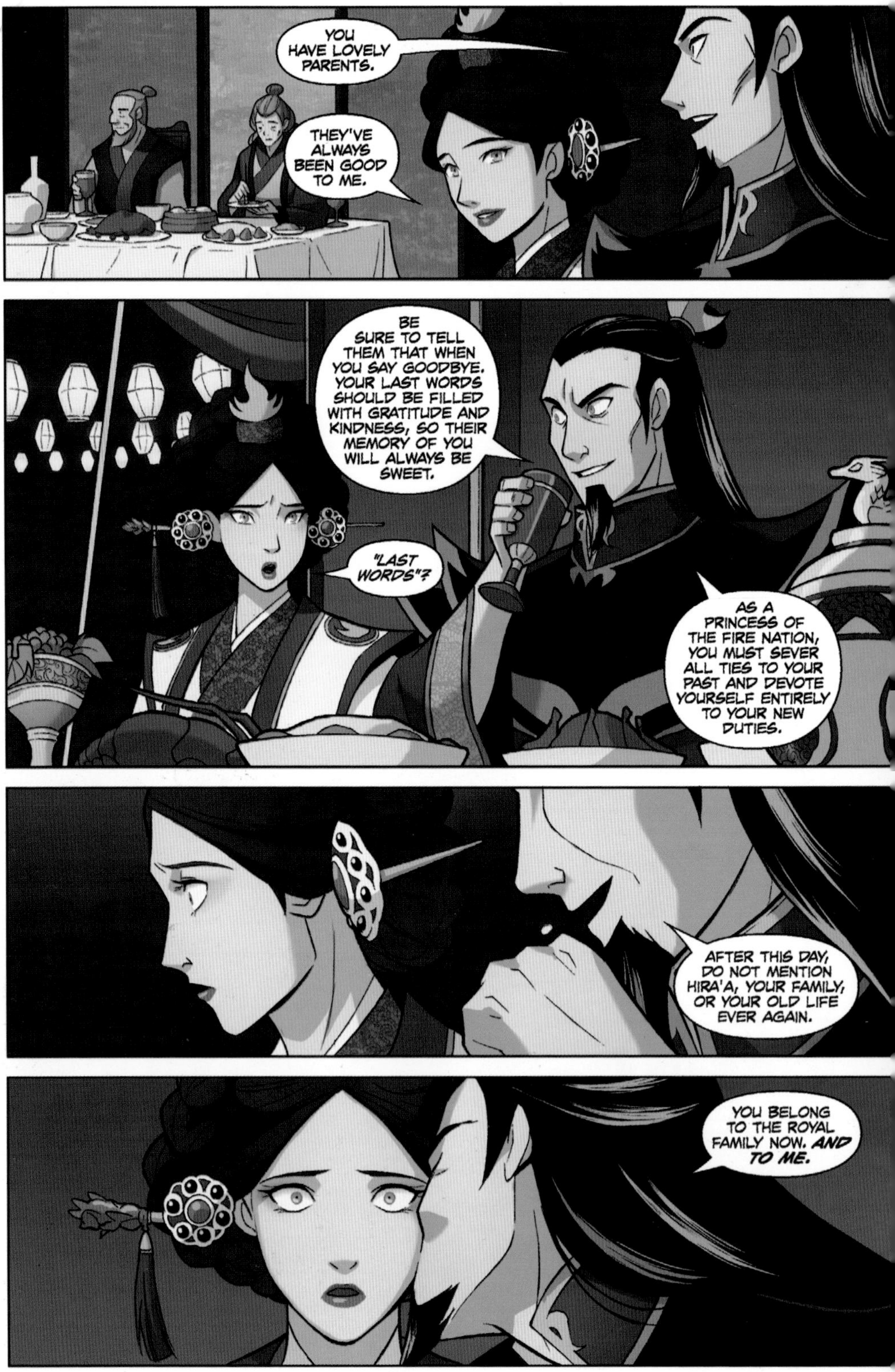
YOU HAVE LOVELY PARENTS.
THEY'VE ALWAYS BEEN GOOD TO ME.
BE SURE TO TELL THEM THAT WHEN YOU SAY GOODBYE. YOUR LAST WORDS SHOULD BE FILLED WITH GRATITUDE AND KINDNESS, SO THEIR MEMORY OF YOU WILL ALWAYS BE SWEET.
"LAST WORDS"?
AS A PRINCESS OF THE FIRE NATION, YOU MUST SEVER ALL TIES TO YOUR PAST AND DEVOTE YOURSELF ENTIRELY TO YOUR NEW DUTIES.
AFTER THIS DAY, DO NOT MENTION HIRA'A, YOUR FAMILY, OR YOUR OLD LIFE EVER AGAIN.
YOU BELONG TO THE ROYAL FAMILY NOW. ***AND TO ME.***

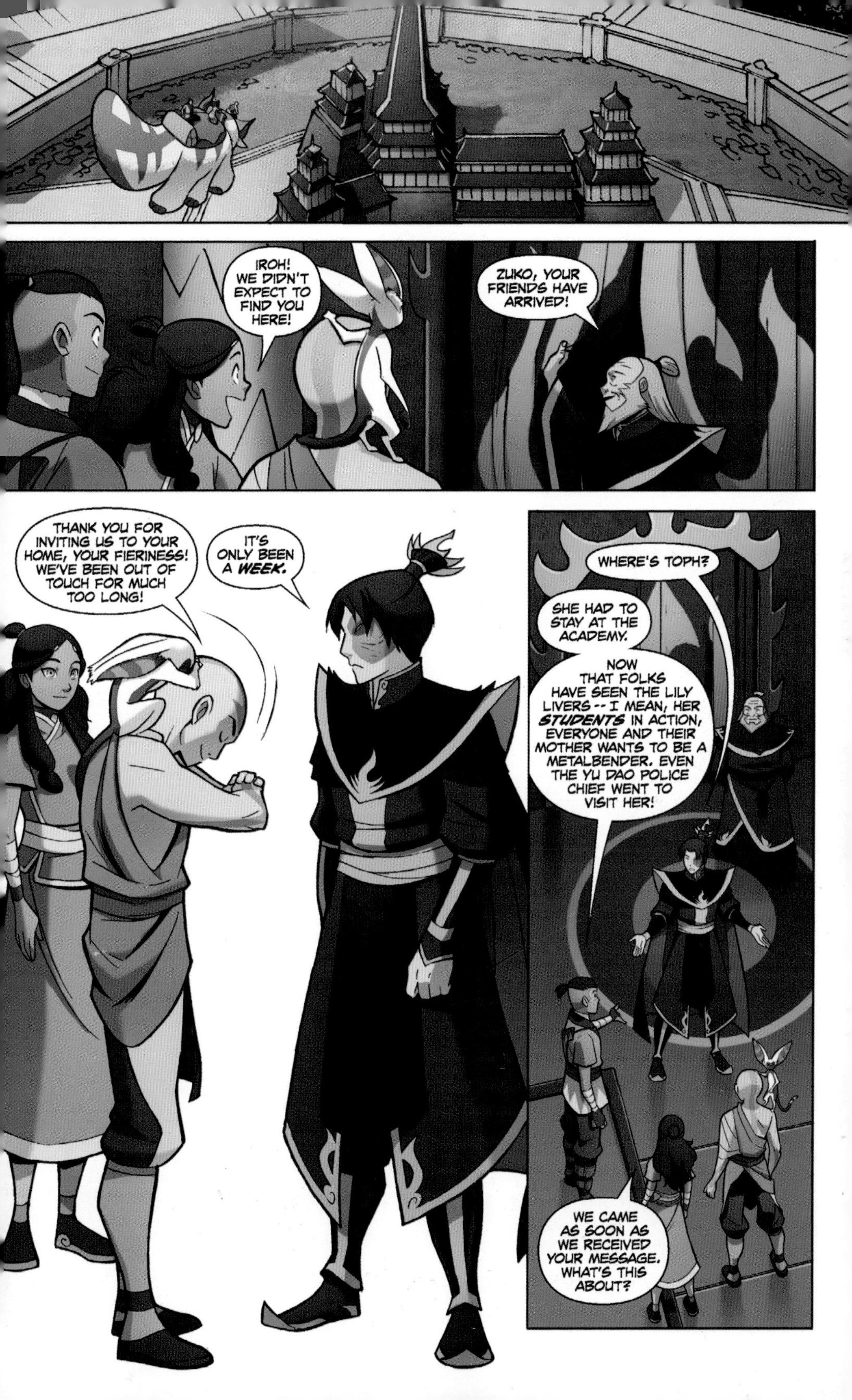
IROH! WE DIDN'T EXPECT TO FIND YOU HERE!
ZUKO, YOUR FRIENDS HAVE ARRIVED!
THANK YOU FOR INVITING US TO YOUR HOME, YOUR FIERINESS! WE'VE BEEN OUT OF TOUCH FOR MUCH TOO LONG!
IT'S ONLY BEEN A **WEEK.**
WHERE'S TOPH?
SHE HAD TO STAY AT THE ACADEMY.
NOW THAT FOLKS HAVE SEEN THE LILY LIVERS -- I MEAN, HER **STUDENTS** IN ACTION, EVERYONE AND THEIR MOTHER WANTS TO BE A METALBENDER. EVEN THE YU DAO POLICE CHIEF WENT TO VISIT HER!
WE CAME AS SOON AS WE RECEIVED YOUR MESSAGE. WHAT'S THIS ABOUT?

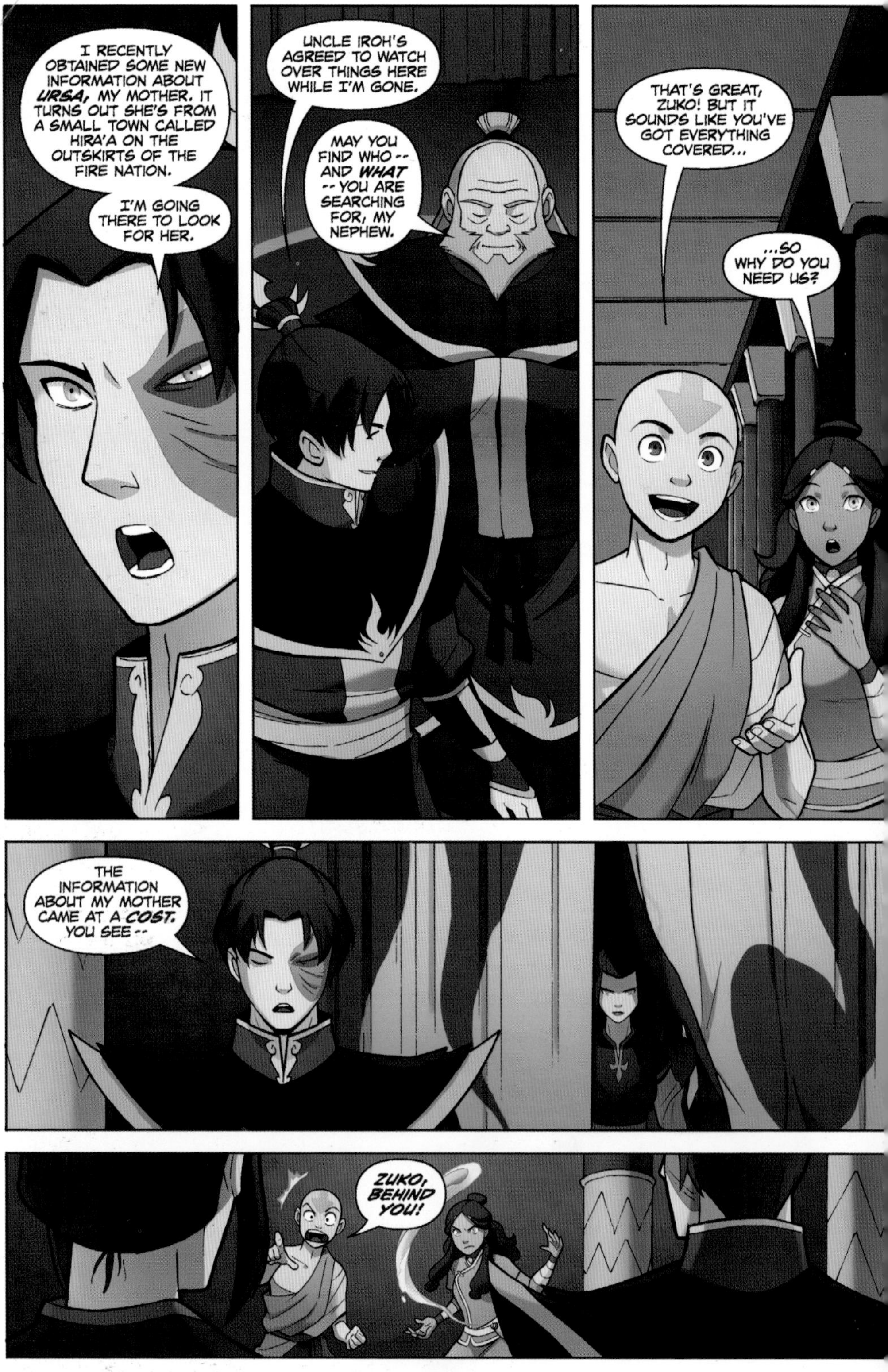
I RECENTLY OBTAINED SOME NEW INFORMATION ABOUT URSA, MY MOTHER. IT TURNS OUT SHE'S FROM A SMALL TOWN CALLED HIRA'A ON THE OUTSKIRTS OF THE FIRE NATION.
I'M GOING THERE TO LOOK FOR HER.
UNCLE IROH'S AGREED TO WATCH OVER THINGS HERE WHILE I'M GONE.
MAY YOU FIND WHO -- AND WHAT -- YOU ARE SEARCHING FOR, MY NEPHEW.
THAT'S GREAT, ZUKO! BUT IT SOUNDS LIKE YOU'VE GOT EVERYTHING COVERED...
...SO WHY DO YOU NEED US?
THE INFORMATION ABOUT MY MOTHER CAME AT A COST. YOU SEE --
ZUKO, BEHIND YOU!

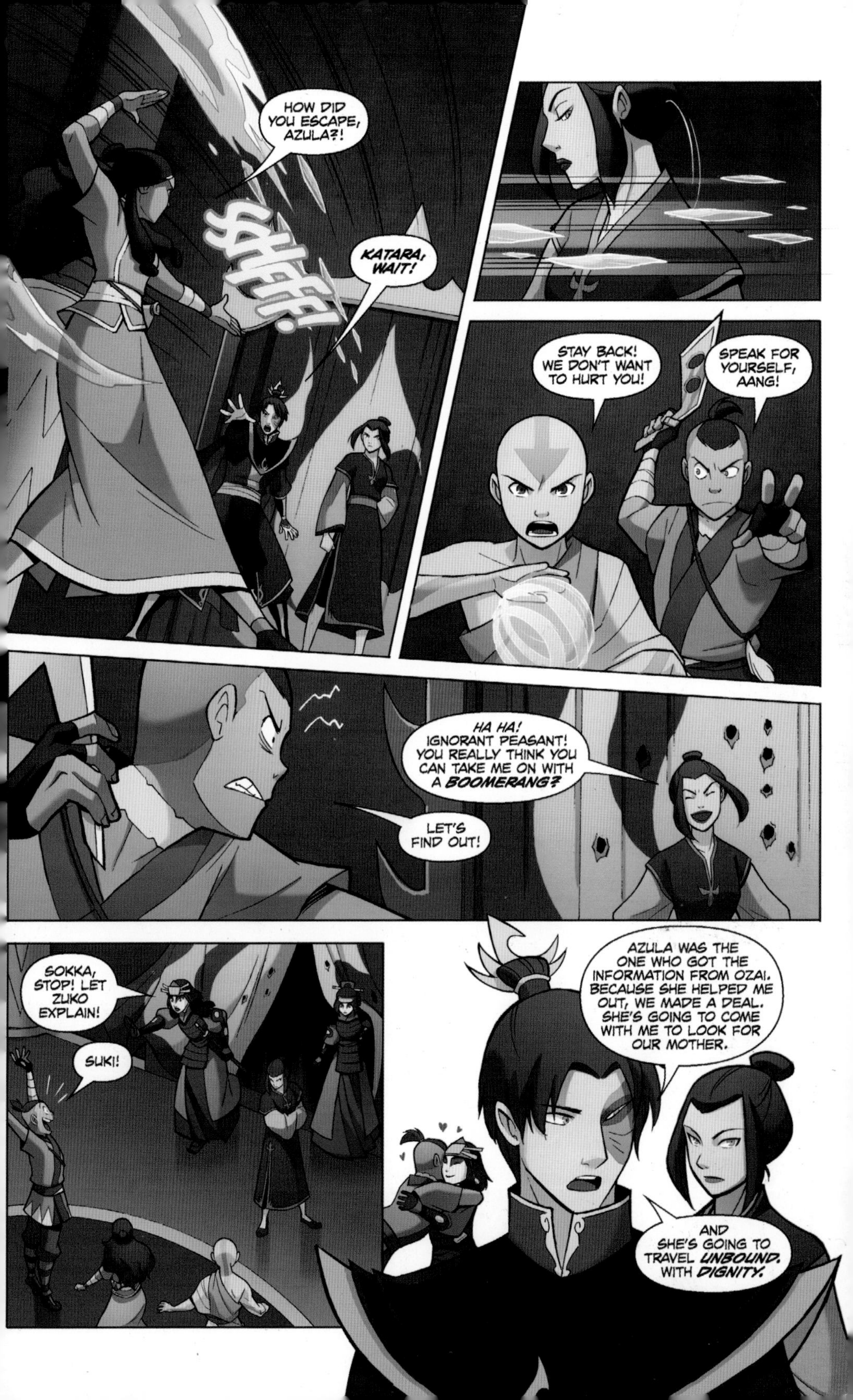
HOW DID YOU ESCAPE, AZULA?!
SHFFF!
KATARA, WAIT!
STAY BACK! WE DON'T WANT TO HURT YOU!
SPEAK FOR YOURSELF, AANG!
HA HA! IGNORANT PEASANT! YOU REALLY THINK YOU CAN TAKE ME ON WITH A BOOMERANG?
LET'S FIND OUT!
SOKKA, STOP! LET ZUKO EXPLAIN!
SUKI!
AZULA WAS THE ONE WHO GOT THE INFORMATION FROM OZAI. BECAUSE SHE HELPED ME OUT, WE MADE A DEAL. SHE'S GOING TO COME WITH ME TO LOOK FOR OUR MOTHER.
AND SHE'S GOING TO TRAVEL UNBOUND. WITH DIGNITY.

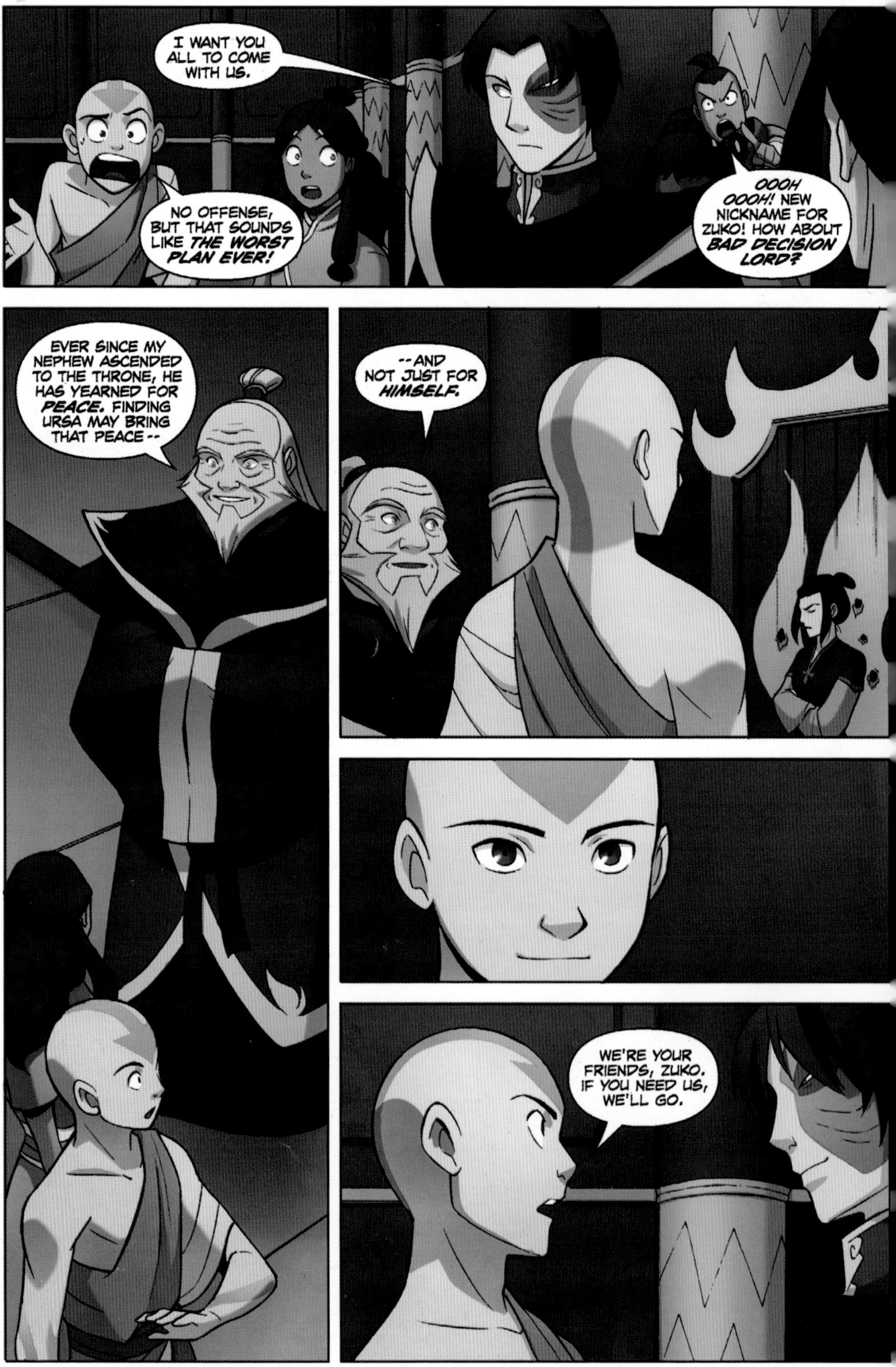
I WANT YOU ALL TO COME WITH US.
NO OFFENSE, BUT THAT SOUNDS LIKE THE WORST PLAN EVER!
OOOH OOOH! NEW NICKNAME FOR ZUKO! HOW ABOUT BAD DECISION LORD?
EVER SINCE MY NEPHEW ASCENDED TO THE THRONE, HE HAS YEARNED FOR PEACE. FINDING URSA MAY BRING THAT PEACE --
--AND NOT JUST FOR HIMSELF.
WE'RE YOUR FRIENDS, ZUKO. IF YOU NEED US, WE'LL GO.

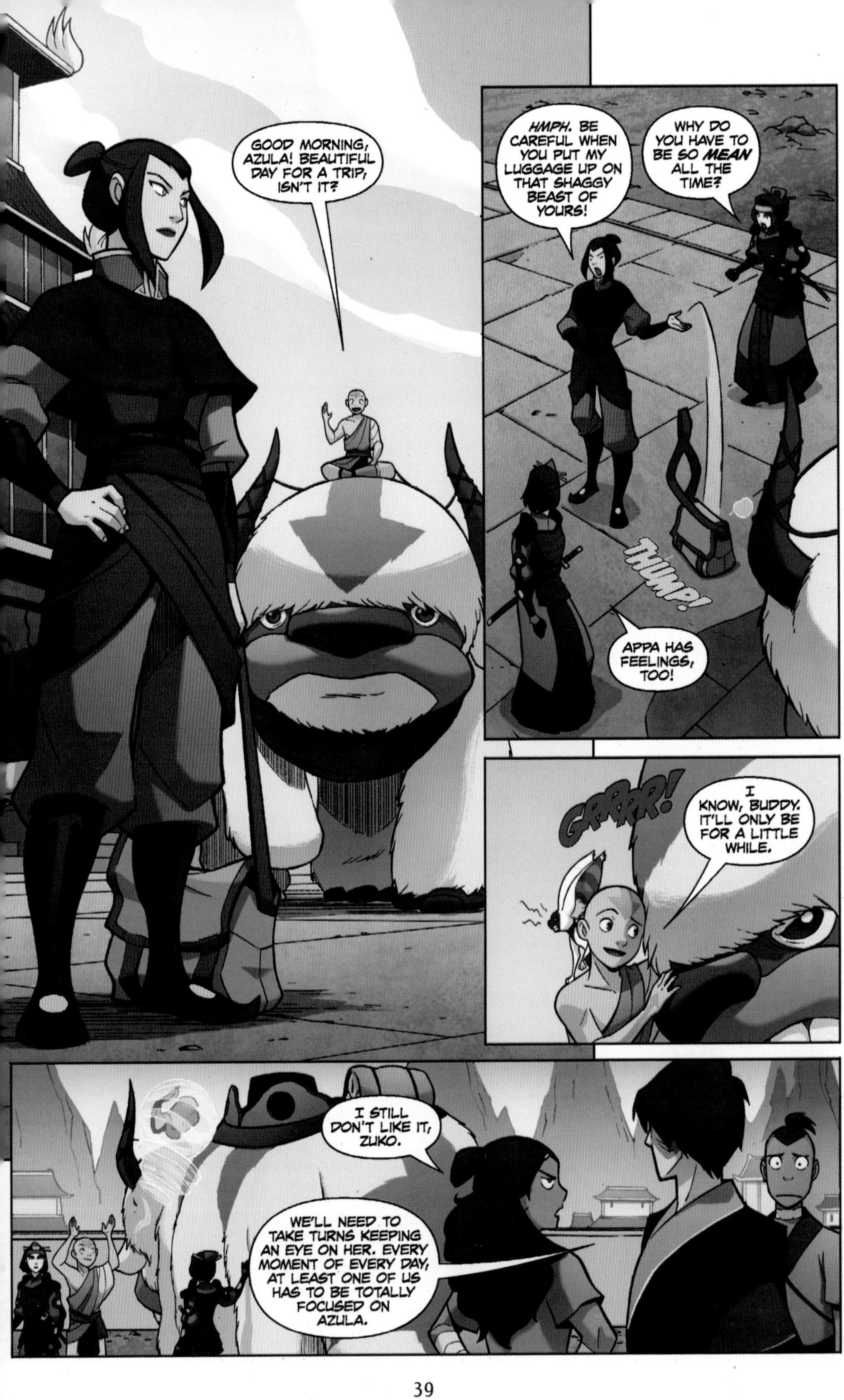
GOOD MORNING, AZULA! BEAUTIFUL DAY FOR A TRIP, ISN'T IT?
HMPH. BE CAREFUL WHEN YOU PUT MY LUGGAGE UP ON THAT SHAGGY BEAST OF YOURS!
WHY DO YOU HAVE TO BE SO MEAN ALL THE TIME?
THUMP!
APPA HAS FEELINGS, TOO!
GRRRR!
I KNOW, BUDDY. IT'LL ONLY BE FOR A LITTLE WHILE.
I STILL DON'T LIKE IT, ZUKO.
WE'LL NEED TO TAKE TURNS KEEPING AN EYE ON HER. EVERY MOMENT OF EVERY DAY, AT LEAST ONE OF US HAS TO BE TOTALLY FOCUSED ON AZULA.

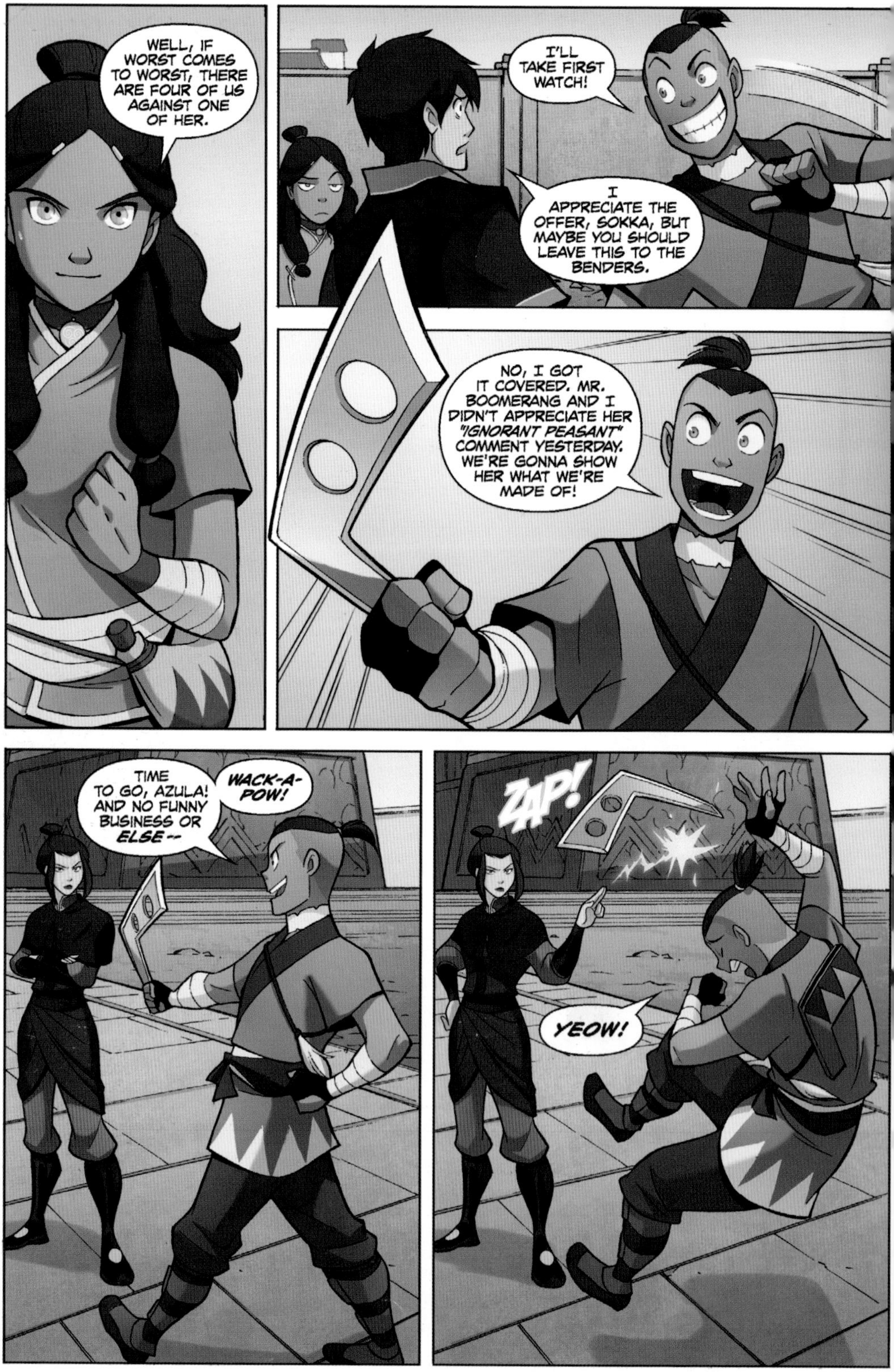
WELL, IF WORST COMES TO WORST, THERE ARE FOUR OF US AGAINST ONE OF HER.
I'LL TAKE FIRST WATCH!
I APPRECIATE THE OFFER, SOKKA, BUT MAYBE YOU SHOULD LEAVE THIS TO THE BENDERS.
NO, I GOT IT COVERED. MR. BOOMERANG AND I DIDN'T APPRECIATE HER "IGNORANT PEASANT" COMMENT YESTERDAY. WE'RE GONNA SHOW HER WHAT WE'RE MADE OF!
TIME TO GO, AZULA! AND NO FUNNY BUSINESS OR ELSE--
WACK-A-POW!
ZAP!
YEOW!

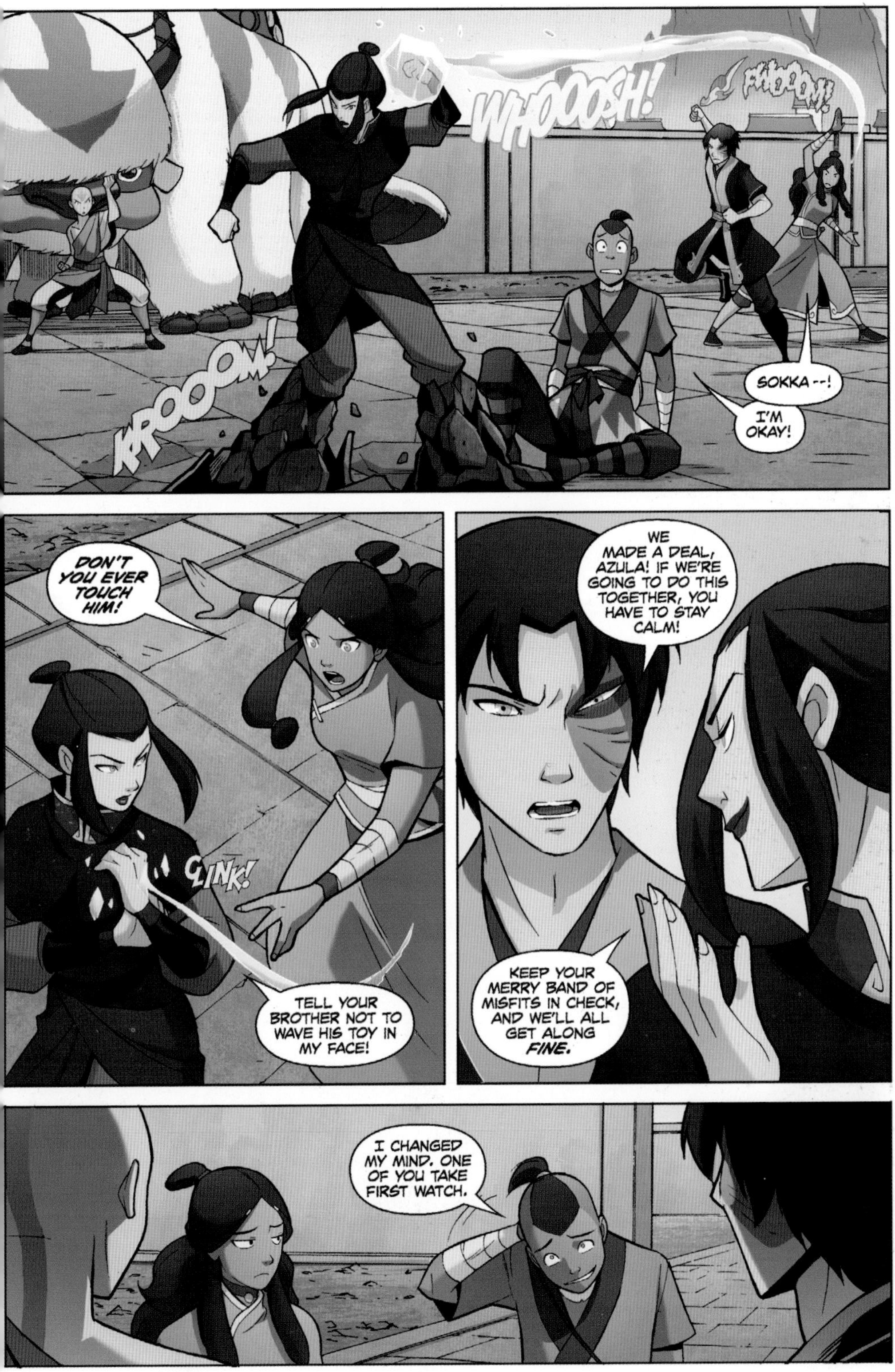
WHOOOSH!
FWOOOM!
KROOOM!
SOKKA --!
I'M OKAY!
DON'T YOU EVER TOUCH HIM!
CLINK!
TELL YOUR BROTHER NOT TO WAVE HIS TOY IN MY FACE!
WE MADE A DEAL, AZULA! IF WE'RE GOING TO DO THIS TOGETHER, YOU HAVE TO STAY CALM!
KEEP YOUR MERRY BAND OF MISFITS IN CHECK, AND WE'LL ALL GET ALONG *FINE*.
I CHANGED MY MIND. ONE OF YOU TAKE FIRST WATCH.

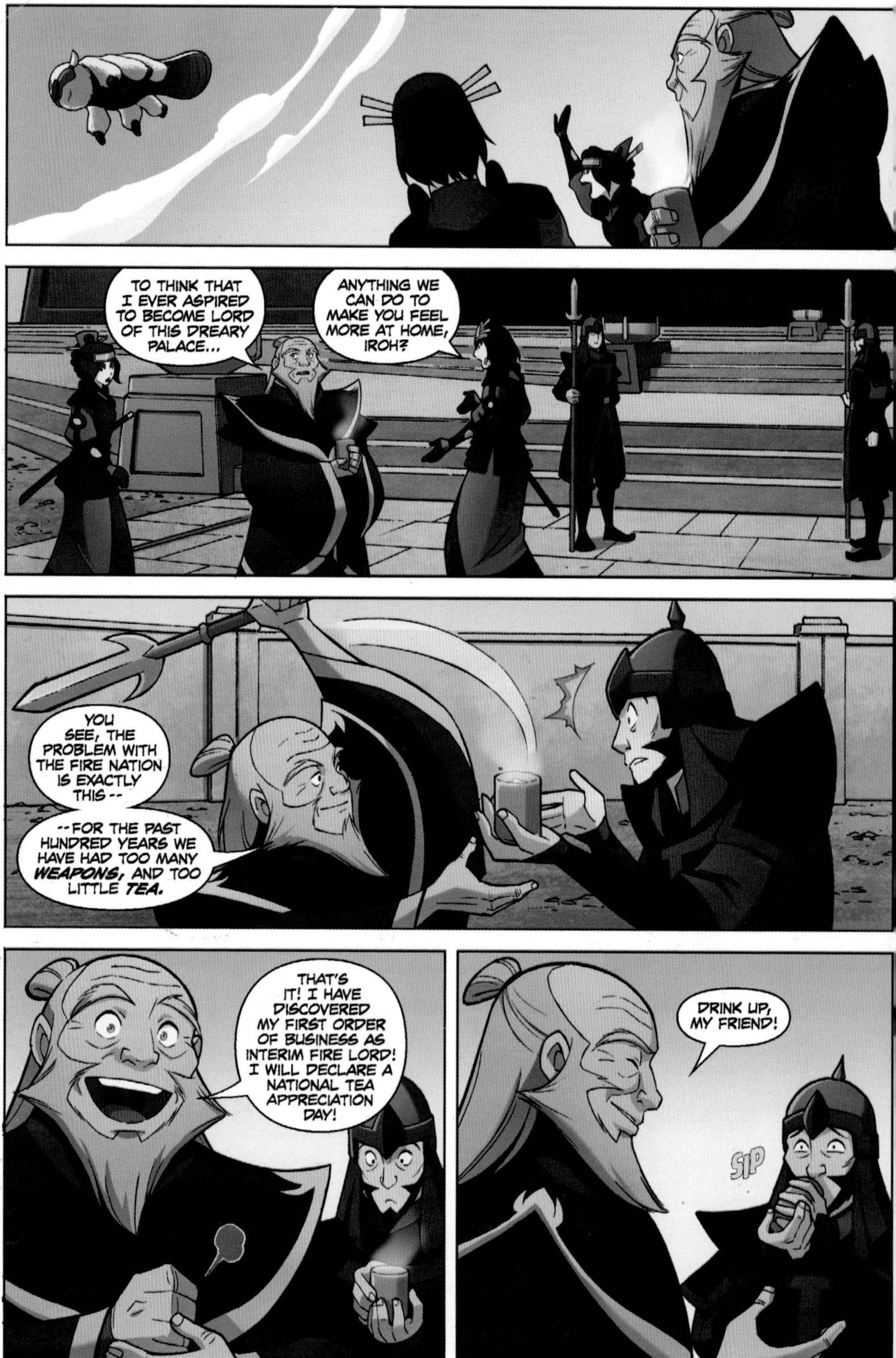
TO THINK THAT I EVER ASPIRED TO BECOME LORD OF THIS DREARY PALACE...
ANYTHING WE CAN DO TO MAKE YOU FEEL MORE AT HOME, IROH?
YOU SEE, THE PROBLEM WITH THE FIRE NATION IS EXACTLY THIS --
--FOR THE PAST HUNDRED YEARS WE HAVE HAD TOO MANY WEAPONS, AND TOO LITTLE TEA.
THAT'S IT! I HAVE DISCOVERED MY FIRST ORDER OF BUSINESS AS INTERIM FIRE LORD! I WILL DECLARE A NATIONAL TEA APPRECIATION DAY!
DRINK UP, MY FRIEND!
SIP

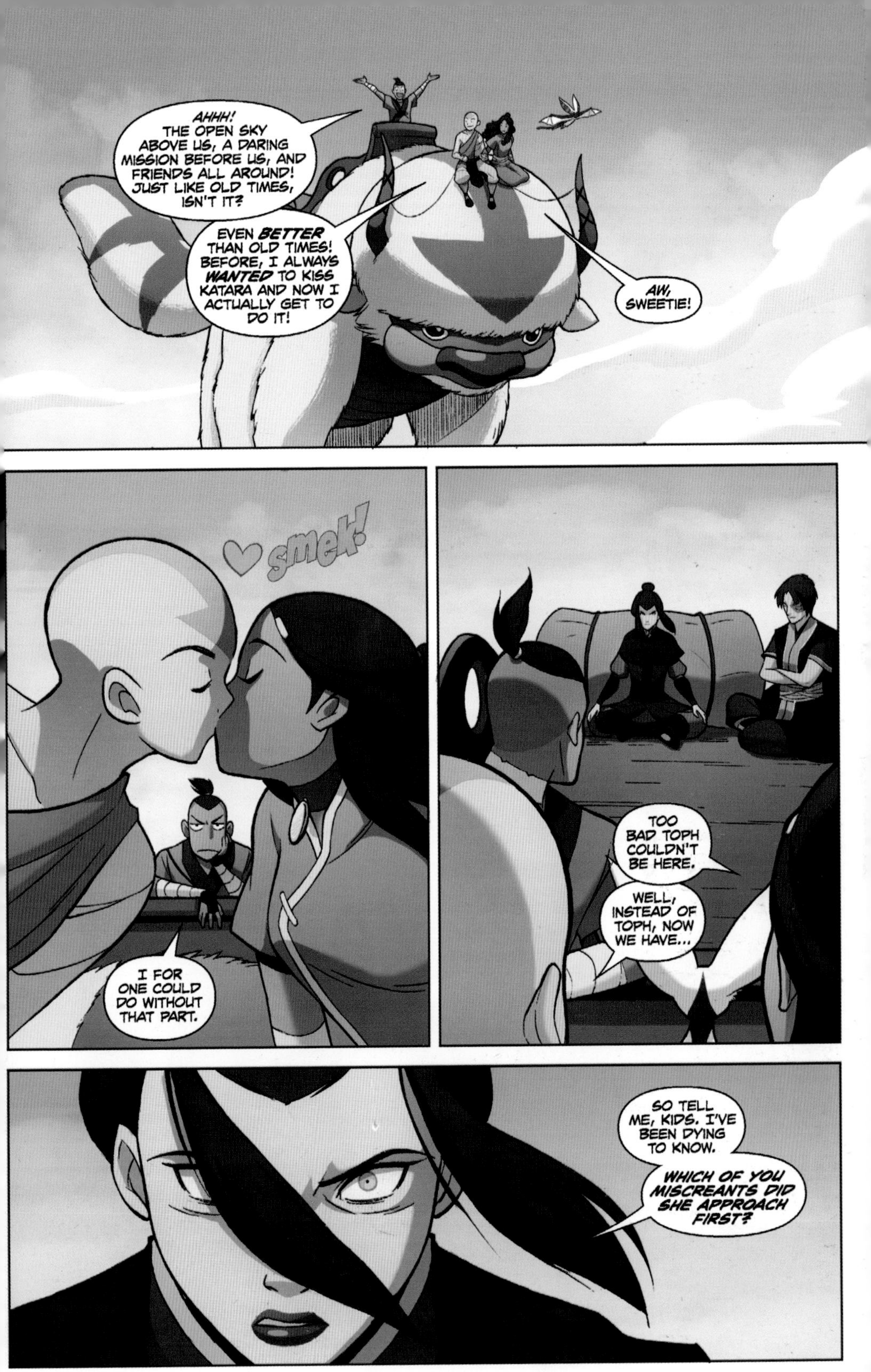
AHHH! THE OPEN SKY ABOVE US, A DARING MISSION BEFORE US, AND FRIENDS ALL AROUND! JUST LIKE OLD TIMES, ISN'T IT?
EVEN BETTER THAN OLD TIMES! BEFORE, I ALWAYS WANTED TO KISS KATARA AND NOW I ACTUALLY GET TO DO IT!
AW, SWEETIE!
smek!
I FOR ONE COULD DO WITHOUT THAT PART.
TOO BAD TOPH COULDN'T BE HERE.
WELL, INSTEAD OF TOPH, NOW WE HAVE...
SO TELL ME, KIDS. I'VE BEEN DYING TO KNOW.
WHICH OF YOU MISCREANTS DID SHE APPROACH FIRST?

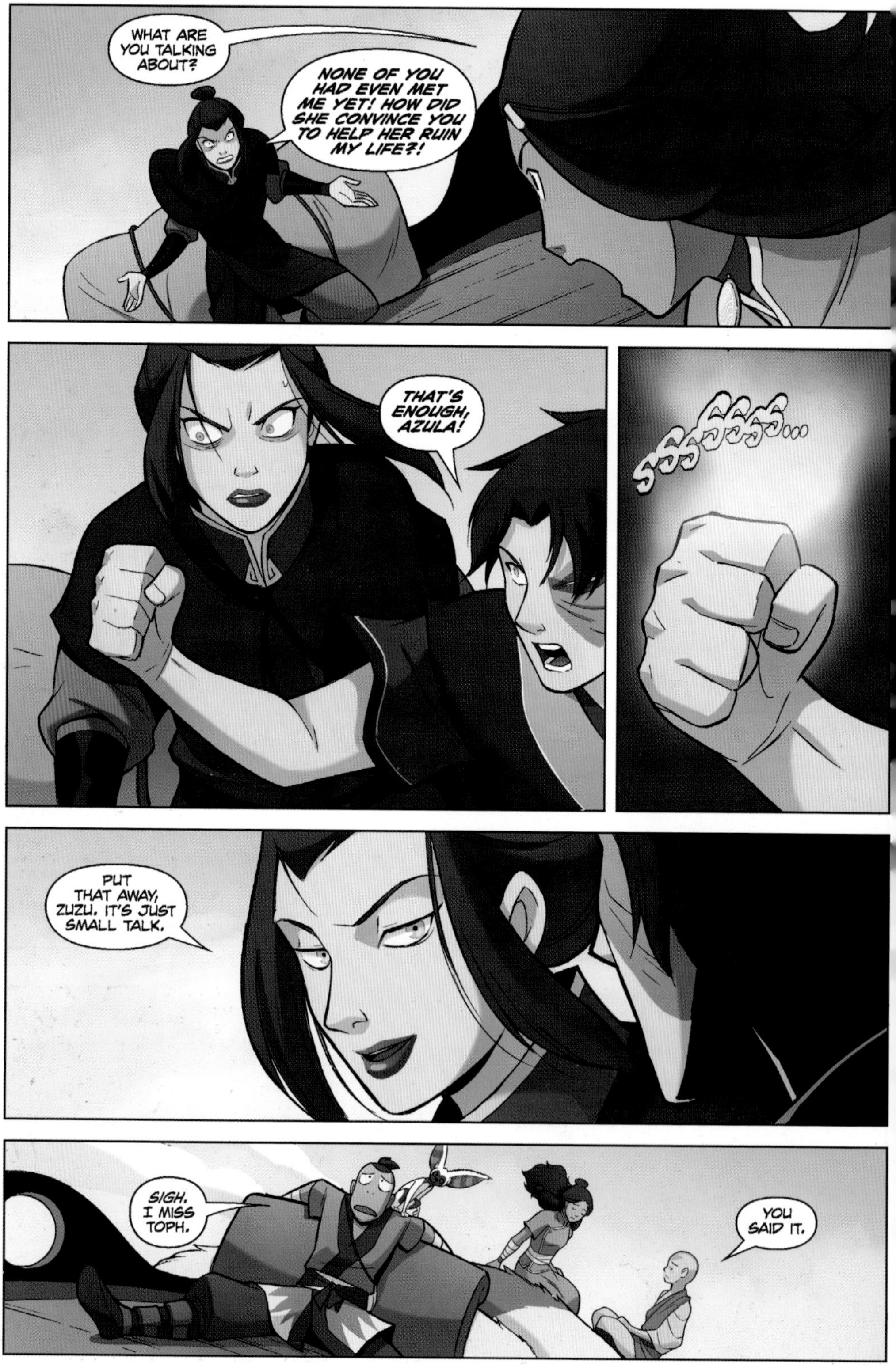
WHAT ARE YOU TALKING ABOUT?
NONE OF YOU HAD EVEN MET ME YET! HOW DID SHE CONVINCE YOU TO HELP HER RUIN MY LIFE?!
THAT'S ENOUGH, AZULA!
SSSSSSS...
PUT THAT AWAY, ZUZU. IT'S JUST SMALL TALK.
SIGH. I MISS TOPH.
YOU SAID IT.

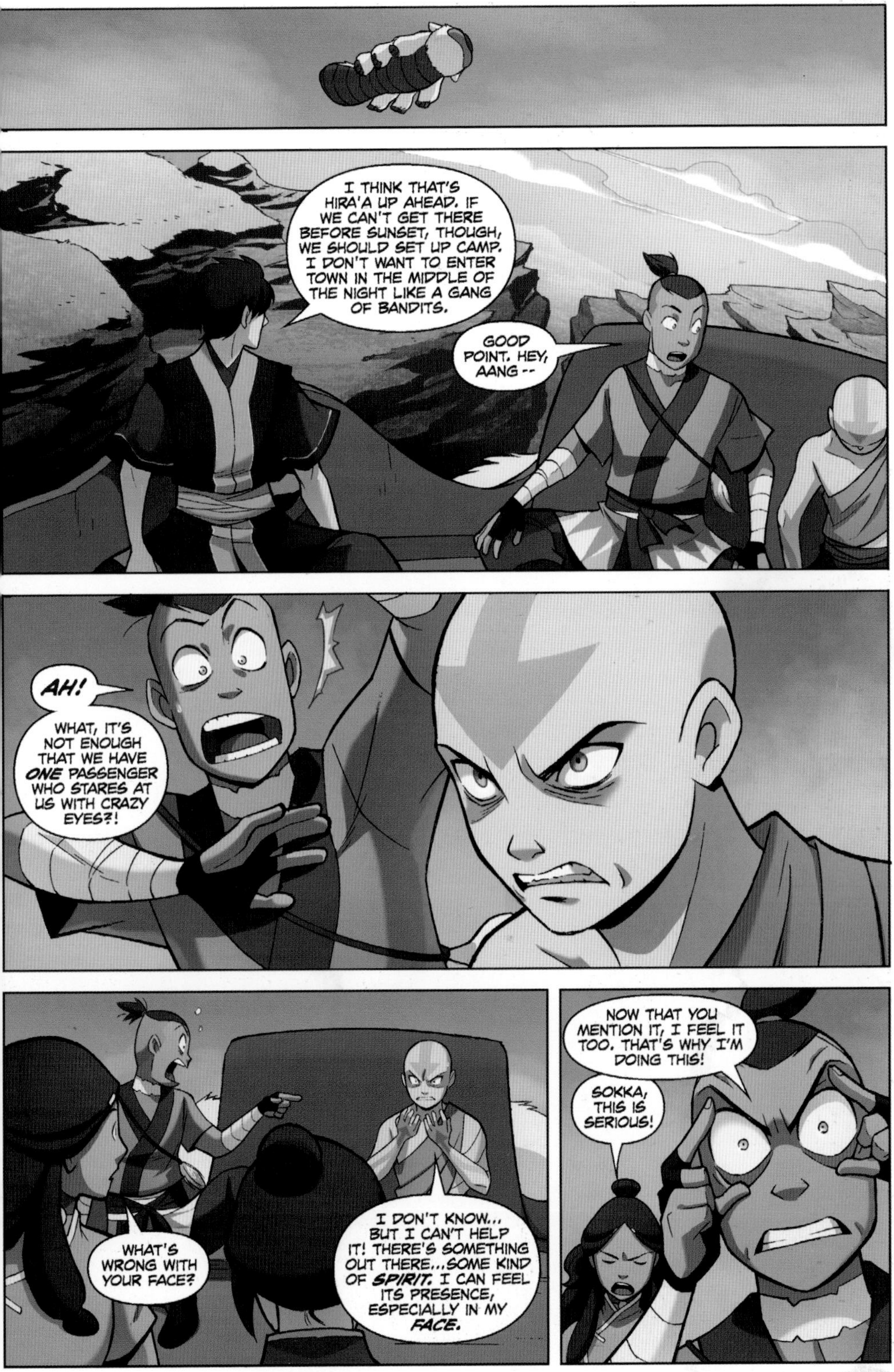
I THINK THAT'S HIRA'A UP AHEAD. IF WE CAN'T GET THERE BEFORE SUNSET, THOUGH, WE SHOULD SET UP CAMP. I DON'T WANT TO ENTER TOWN IN THE MIDDLE OF THE NIGHT LIKE A GANG OF BANDITS.
GOOD POINT. HEY, AANG --
AH!
WHAT, IT'S NOT ENOUGH THAT WE HAVE ONE PASSENGER WHO STARES AT US WITH CRAZY EYES?!
WHAT'S WRONG WITH YOUR FACE?
I DON'T KNOW... BUT I CAN'T HELP IT! THERE'S SOMETHING OUT THERE...SOME KIND OF SPIRIT. I CAN FEEL ITS PRESENCE, ESPECIALLY IN MY FACE.
NOW THAT YOU MENTION IT, I FEEL IT TOO. THAT'S WHY I'M DOING THIS!
SOKKA, THIS IS SERIOUS!

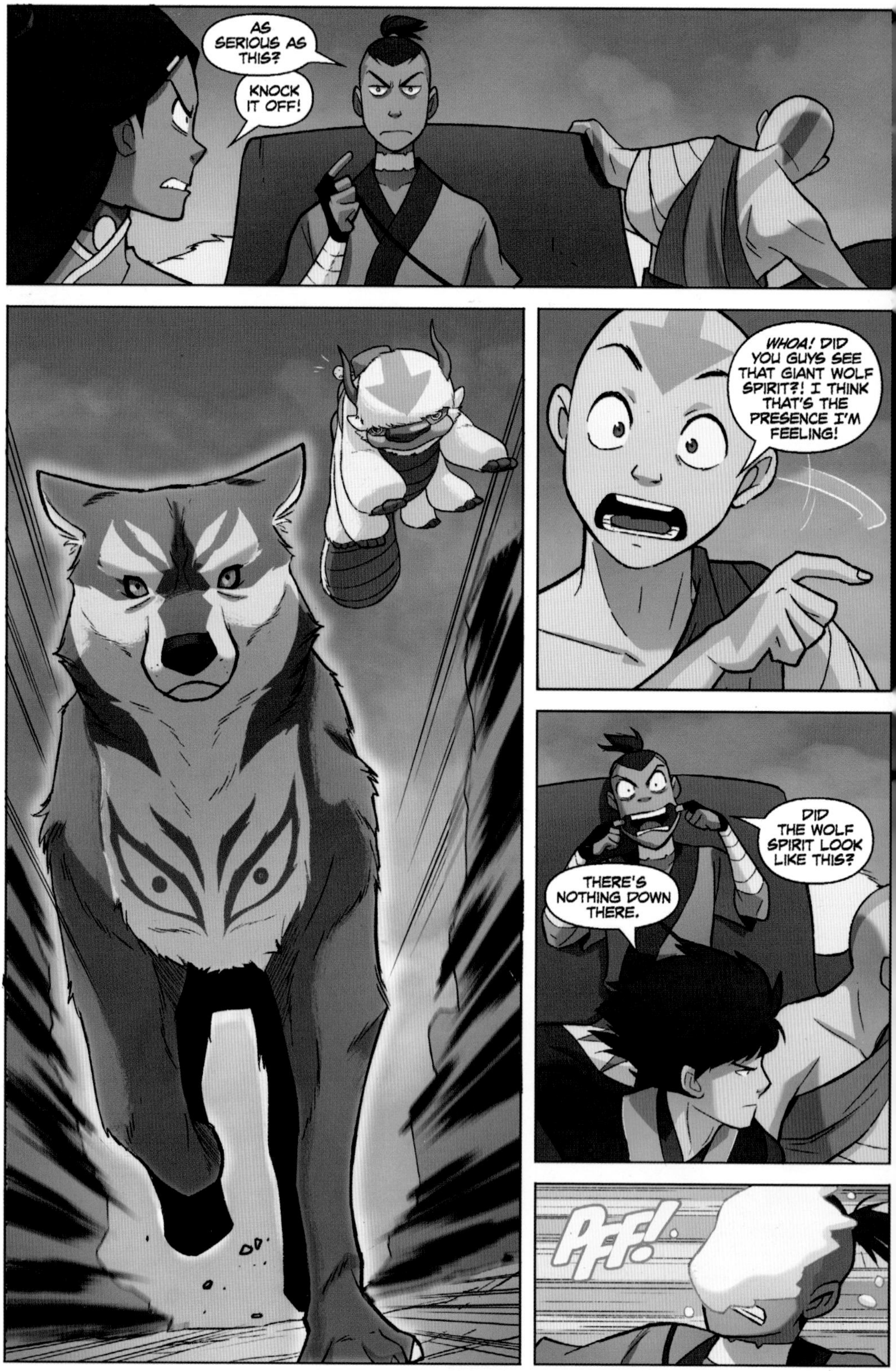
AS SERIOUS AS THIS?
KNOCK IT OFF!
WHOA! DID YOU GUYS SEE THAT GIANT WOLF SPIRIT?! I THINK THAT'S THE PRESENCE I'M FEELING!
DID THE WOLF SPIRIT LOOK LIKE THIS?
THERE'S NOTHING DOWN THERE.
PFF!

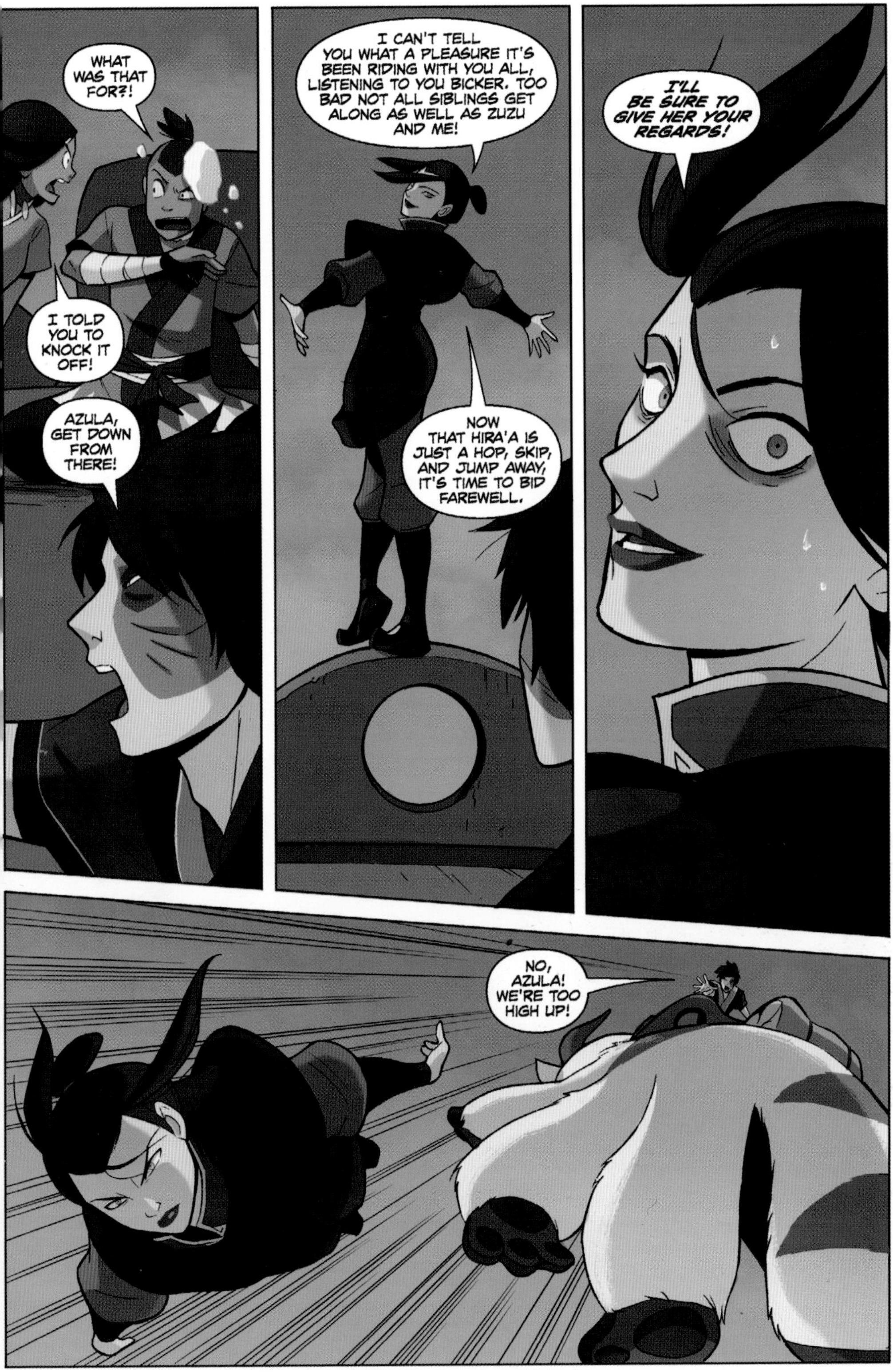
WHAT WAS THAT FOR?!
I TOLD YOU TO KNOCK IT OFF!
AZULA, GET DOWN FROM THERE!
I CAN'T TELL YOU WHAT A PLEASURE IT'S BEEN RIDING WITH YOU ALL, LISTENING TO YOU BICKER. TOO BAD NOT ALL SIBLINGS GET ALONG AS WELL AS ZUZU AND ME!
NOW THAT HIRA'A IS JUST A HOP, SKIP, AND JUMP AWAY, IT'S TIME TO BID FAREWELL.
I'LL BE SURE TO GIVE HER YOUR REGARDS!
NO, AZULA! WE'RE TOO HIGH UP!

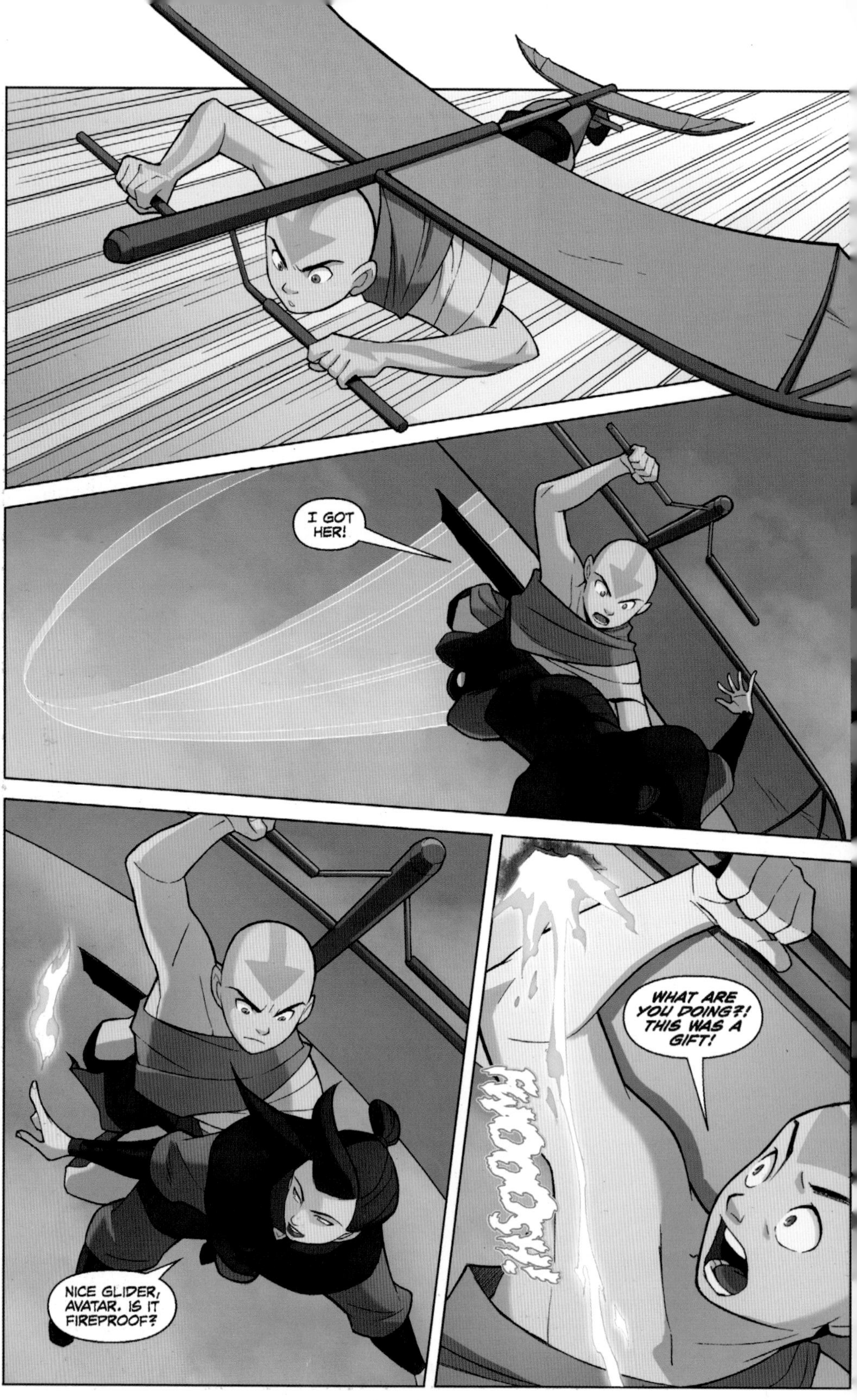
I GOT HER!
NICE GLIDER, AVATAR. IS IT FIREPROOF?
FWOOSH!
WHAT ARE YOU DOING?! THIS WAS A GIFT!

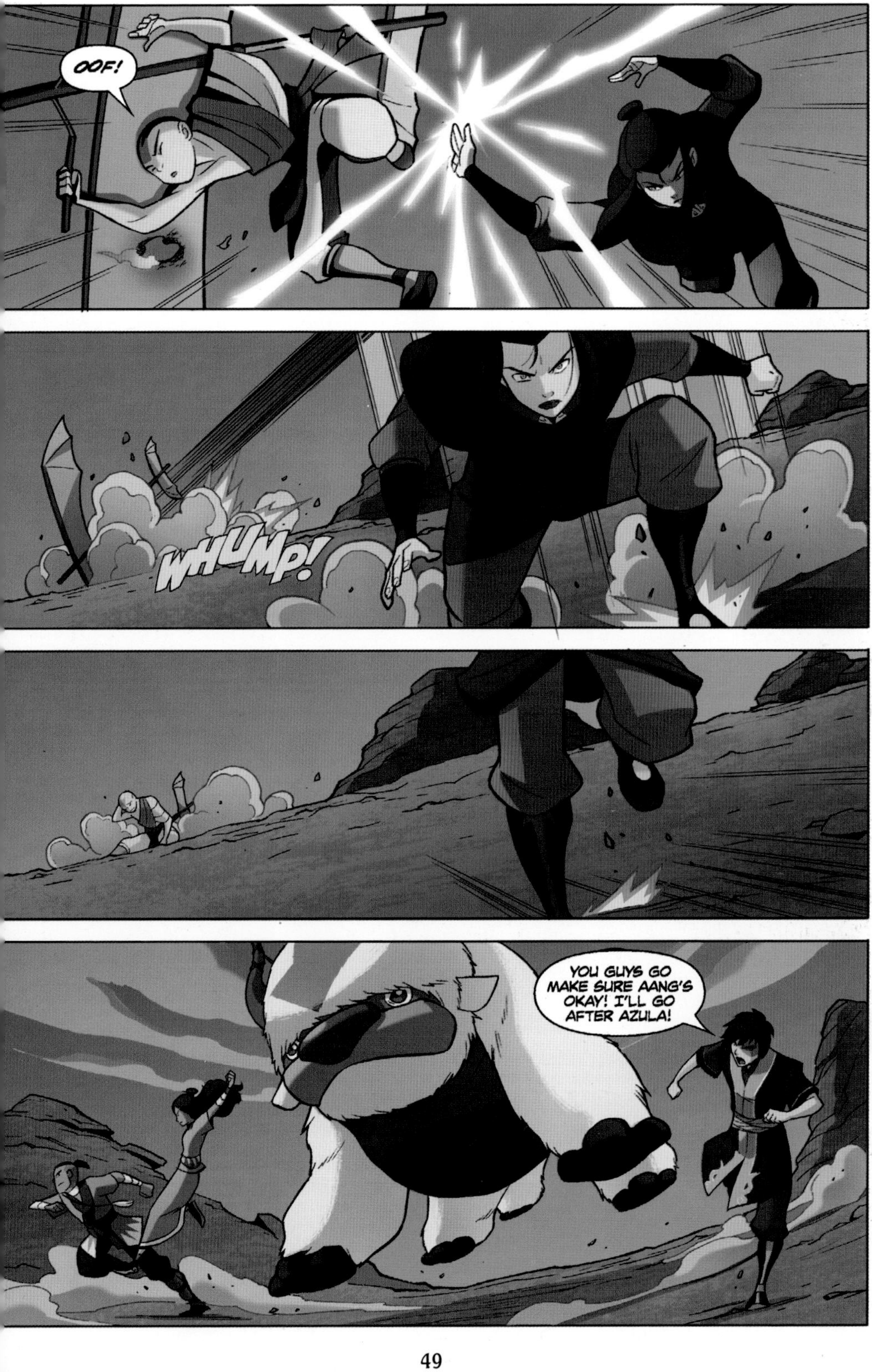
OOF!
WHUMP!
YOU GUYS GO MAKE SURE AANG'S OKAY! I'LL GO AFTER AZULA!

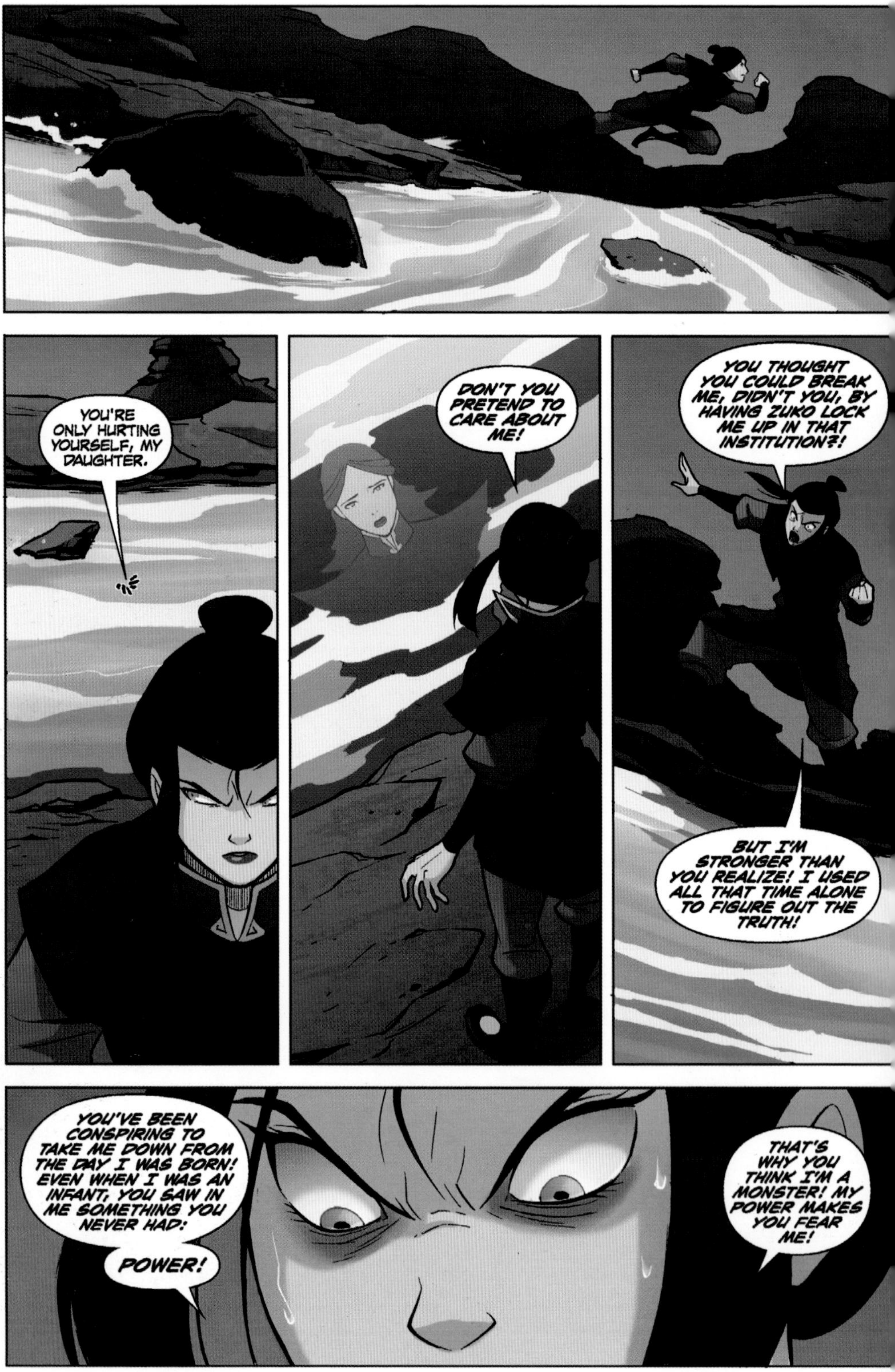
YOU'RE ONLY HURTING YOURSELF, MY DAUGHTER.
DON'T YOU PRETEND TO CARE ABOUT ME!
YOU THOUGHT YOU COULD BREAK ME, DIDN'T YOU, BY HAVING ZUKO LOCK ME UP IN THAT INSTITUTION?!
BUT I'M STRONGER THAN YOU REALIZE! I USED ALL THAT TIME ALONE TO FIGURE OUT THE TRUTH!
YOU'VE BEEN CONSPIRING TO TAKE ME DOWN FROM THE DAY I WAS BORN! EVEN WHEN I WAS AN INFANT, YOU SAW IN ME SOMETHING YOU NEVER HAD:
POWER!
THAT'S WHY YOU THINK I'M A MONSTER! MY POWER MAKES YOU FEAR ME!

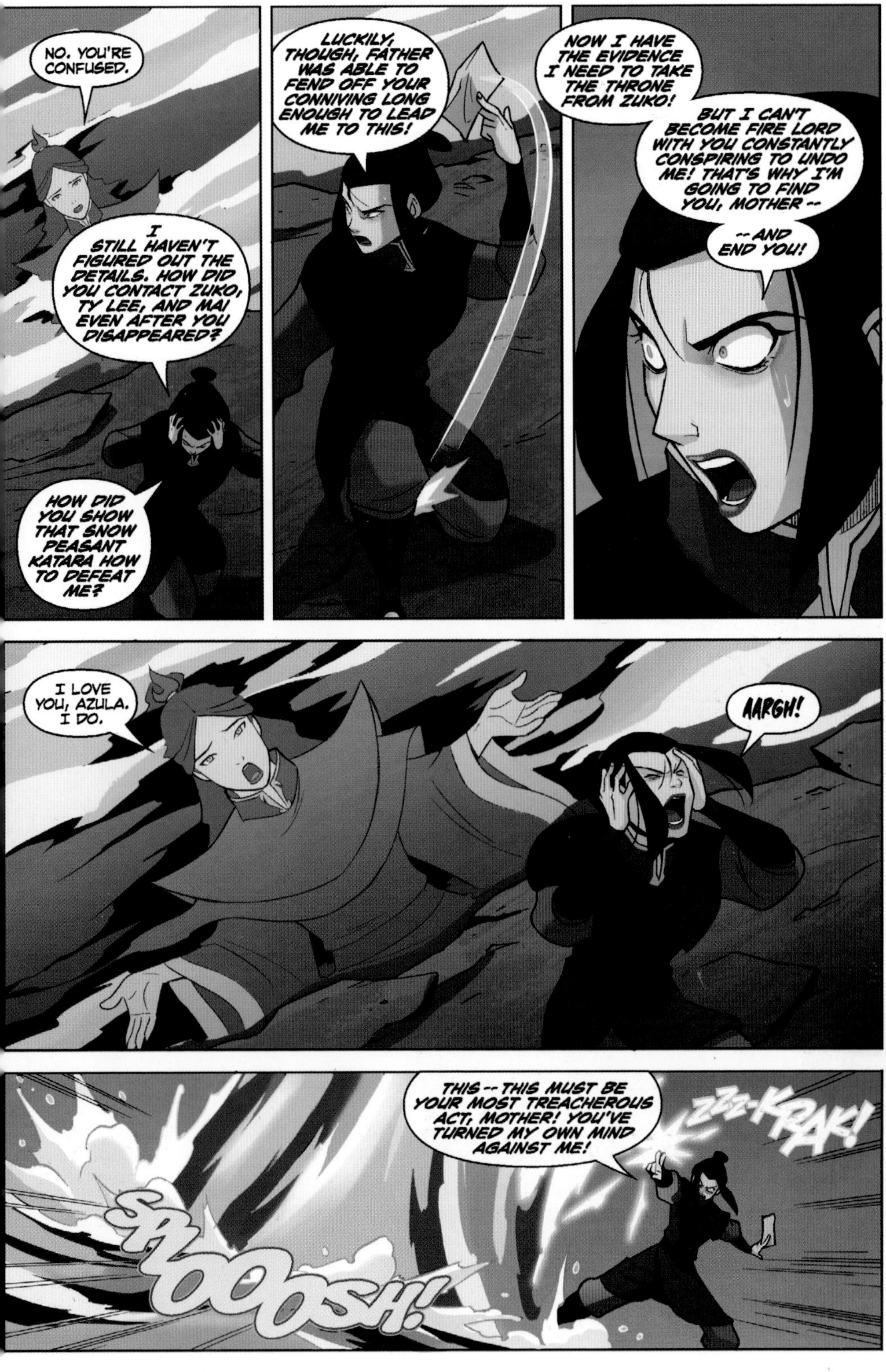
NO. YOU'RE CONFUSED.
I STILL HAVEN'T FIGURED OUT THE DETAILS. HOW DID YOU CONTACT ZUKO, TY LEE, AND MAI EVEN AFTER YOU DISAPPEARED?
HOW DID YOU SHOW THAT SNOW PEASANT KATARA HOW TO DEFEAT ME?
LUCKILY, THOUGH, FATHER WAS ABLE TO FEND OFF YOUR CONNIVING LONG ENOUGH TO LEAD ME TO THIS!
NOW I HAVE THE EVIDENCE I NEED TO TAKE THE THRONE FROM ZUKO!
BUT I CAN'T BECOME FIRE LORD WITH YOU CONSTANTLY CONSPIRING TO UNDO ME! THAT'S WHY I'M GOING TO FIND YOU, MOTHER --
-- AND END YOU!
I LOVE YOU, AZULA. I DO.
AARGH!
THIS -- THIS MUST BE YOUR MOST TREACHEROUS ACT, MOTHER! YOU'VE TURNED MY OWN MIND AGAINST ME!
ZZZ-KRAK!
SPLOOOSH!

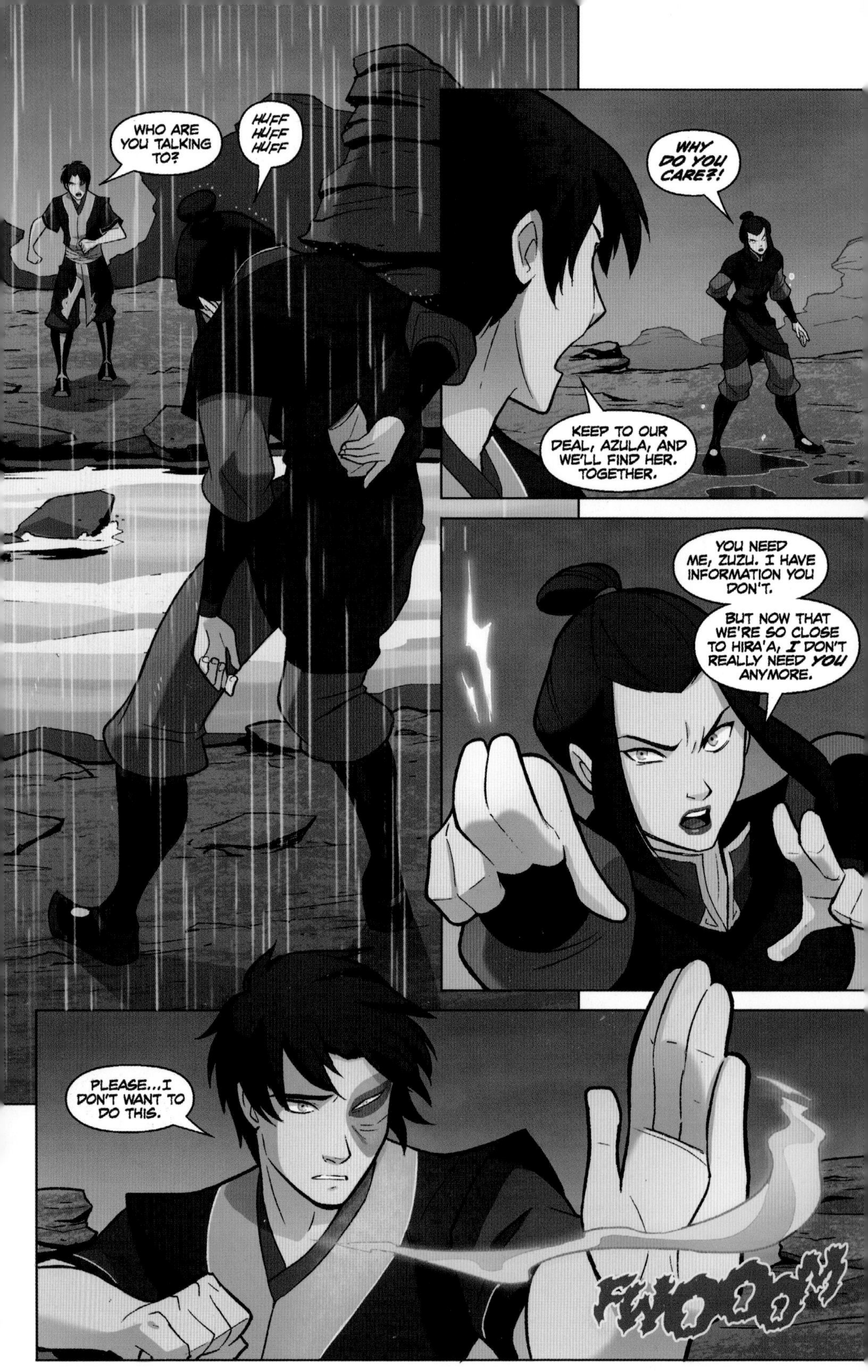
WHO ARE YOU TALKING TO?
HUFF HUFF HUFF
WHY DO YOU CARE?!
KEEP TO OUR DEAL, AZULA, AND WE'LL FIND HER. TOGETHER.
YOU NEED ME, ZUZU. I HAVE INFORMATION YOU DON'T.
BUT NOW THAT WE'RE SO CLOSE TO HIRA'A, I DON'T REALLY NEED YOU ANYMORE.
PLEASE...I DON'T WANT TO DO THIS.
FWOOOM

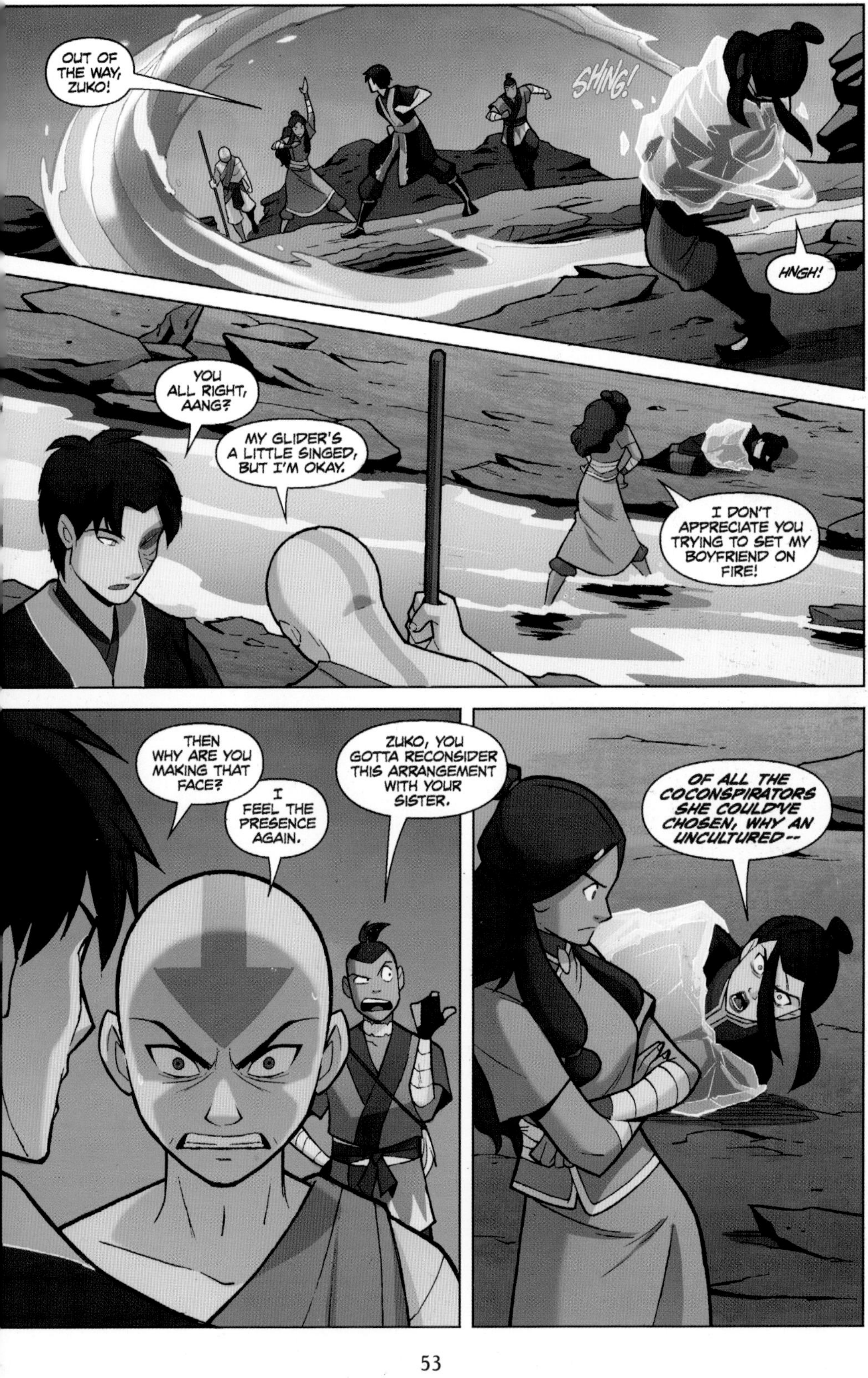
OUT OF THE WAY, ZUKO!
SHING!
HNGH!
YOU ALL RIGHT, AANG?
MY GLIDER'S A LITTLE SINGED, BUT I'M OKAY.
I DON'T APPRECIATE YOU TRYING TO SET MY BOYFRIEND ON FIRE!
THEN WHY ARE YOU MAKING THAT FACE?
I FEEL THE PRESENCE AGAIN.
ZUKO, YOU GOTTA RECONSIDER THIS ARRANGEMENT WITH YOUR SISTER.
OF ALL THE COCONSPIRATORS SHE COULD'VE CHOSEN, WHY AN UNCULTURED--

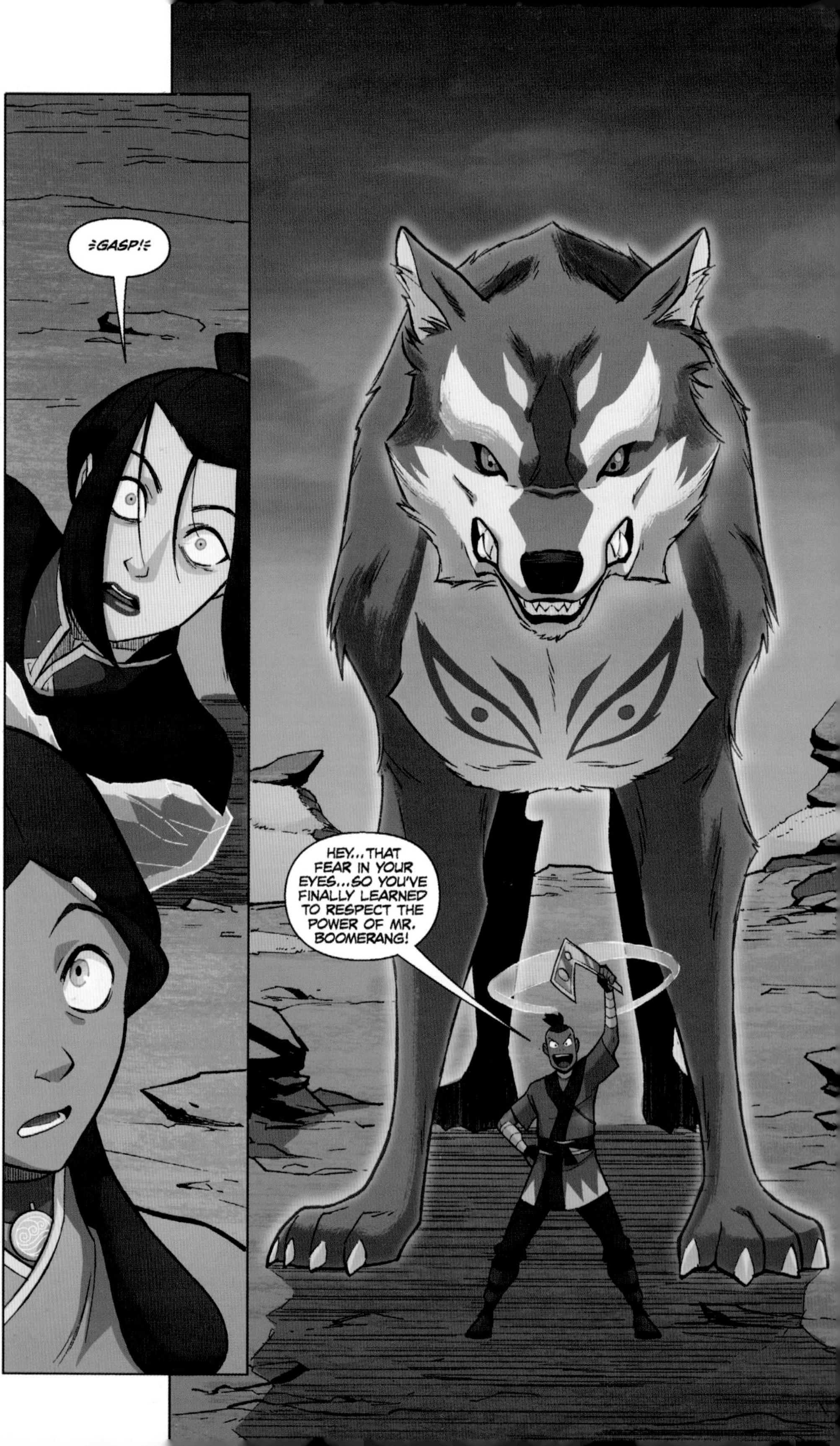

⸗GASP!⸗
HEY... THAT FEAR IN YOUR EYES... SO YOU'VE FINALLY LEARNED TO RESPECT THE POWER OF MR. BOOMERANG!

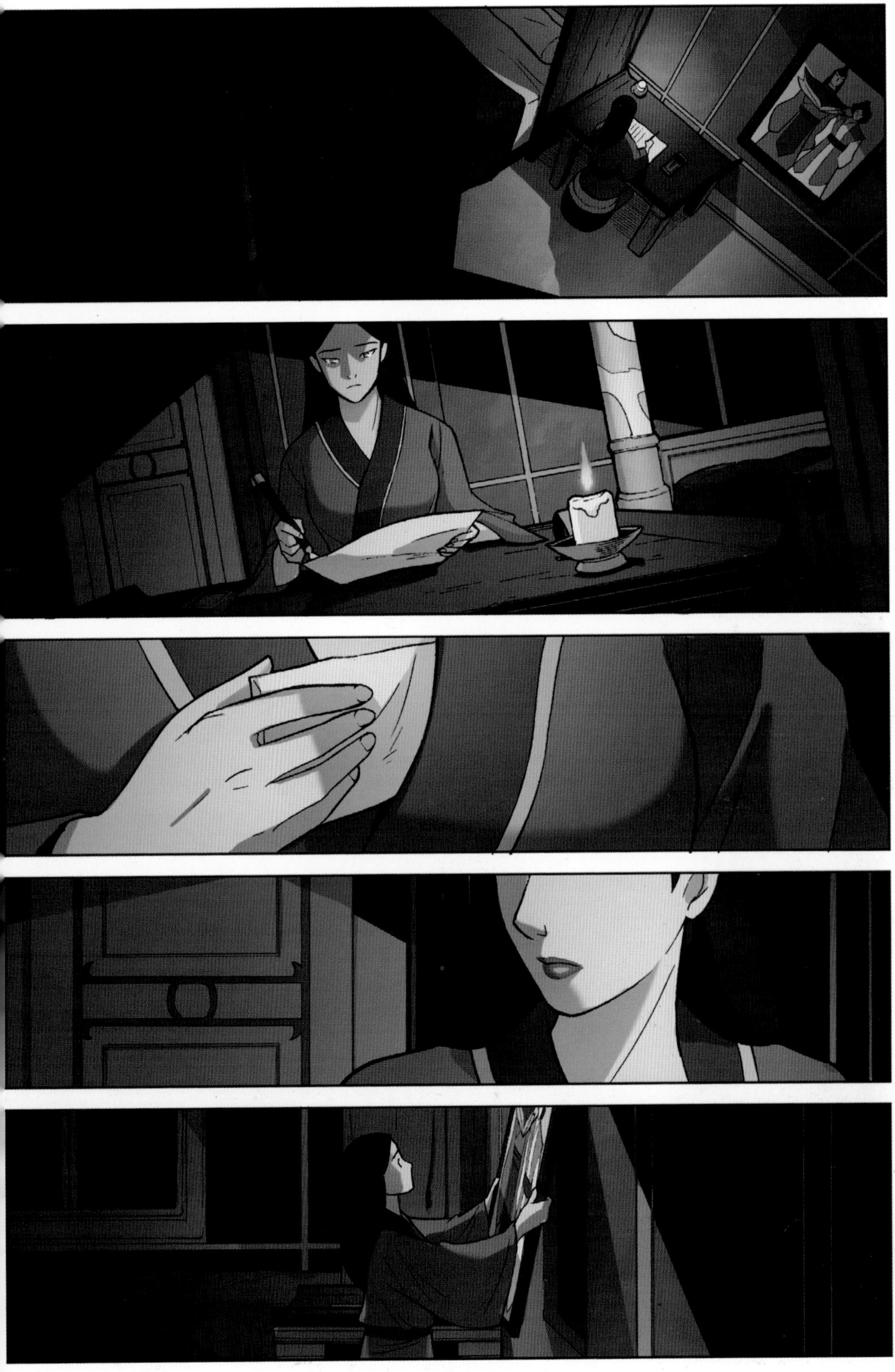

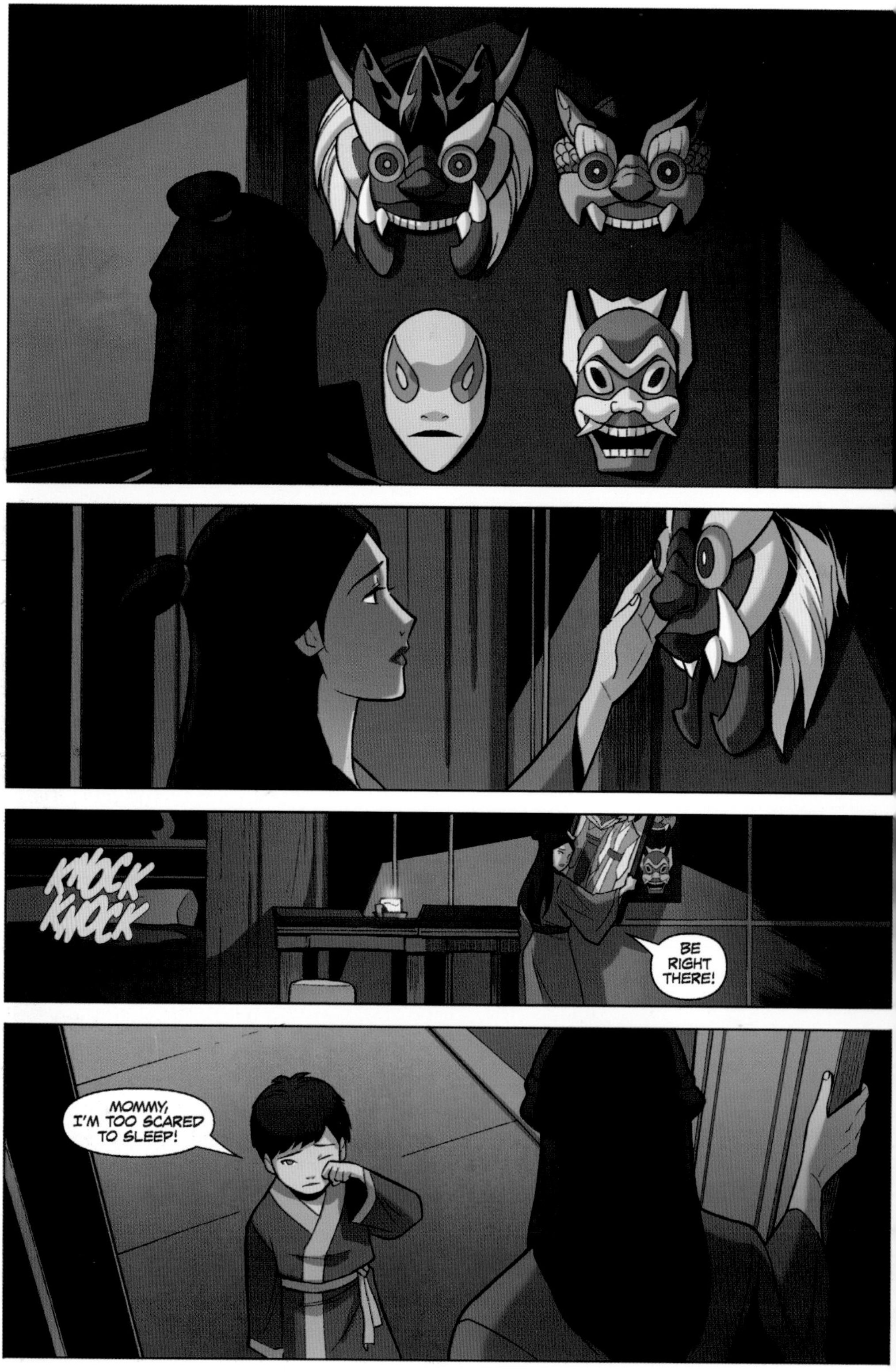
KNOCK KNOCK
BE RIGHT THERE!
MOMMY, I'M TOO SCARED TO SLEEP!

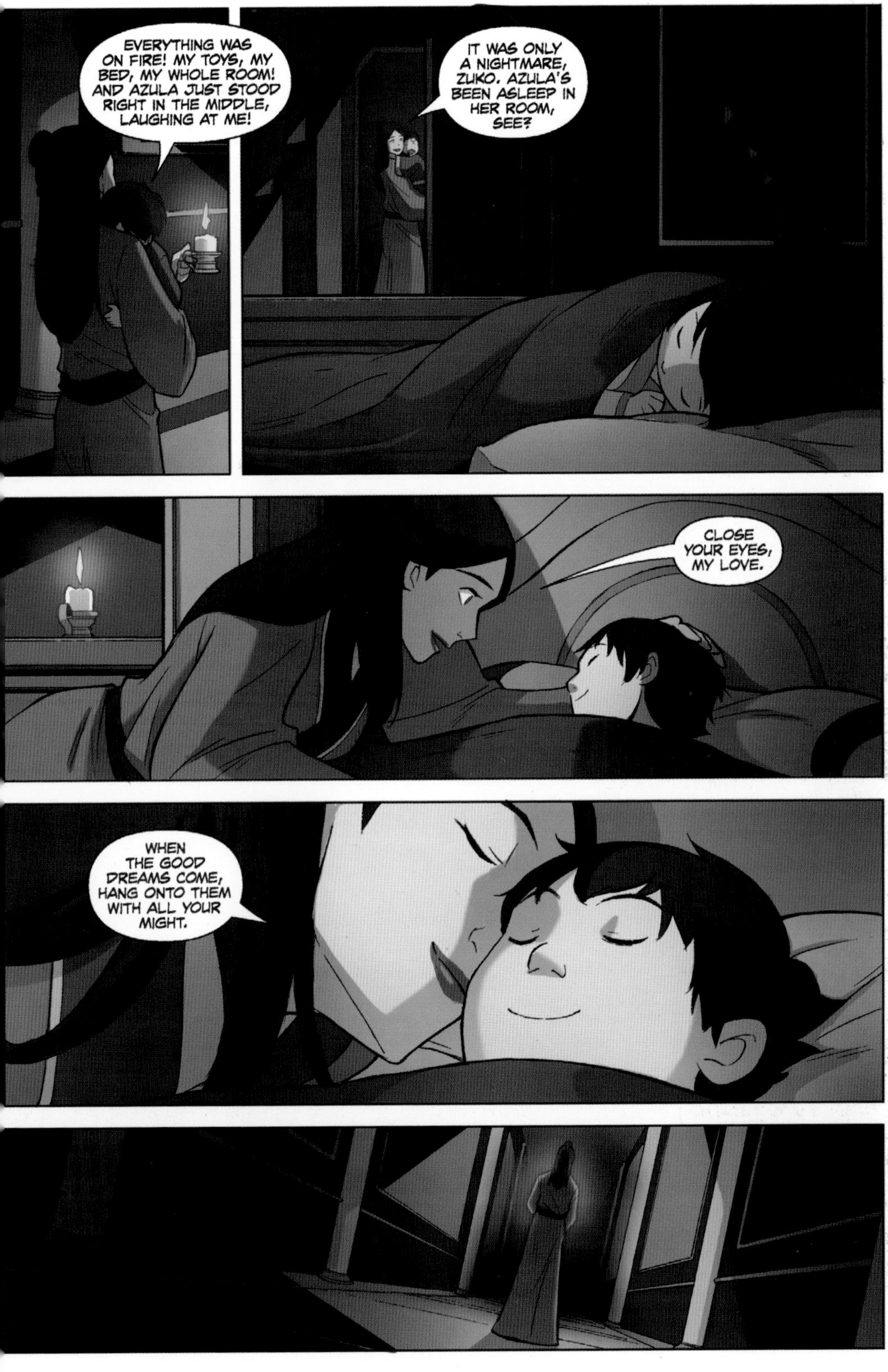
EVERYTHING WAS ON FIRE! MY TOYS, MY BED, MY WHOLE ROOM! AND AZULA JUST STOOD RIGHT IN THE MIDDLE, LAUGHING AT ME!
IT WAS ONLY A NIGHTMARE, ZUKO. AZULA'S BEEN ASLEEP IN HER ROOM, SEE?
CLOSE YOUR EYES, MY LOVE.
WHEN THE GOOD DREAMS COME, HANG ONTO THEM WITH ALL YOUR MIGHT.

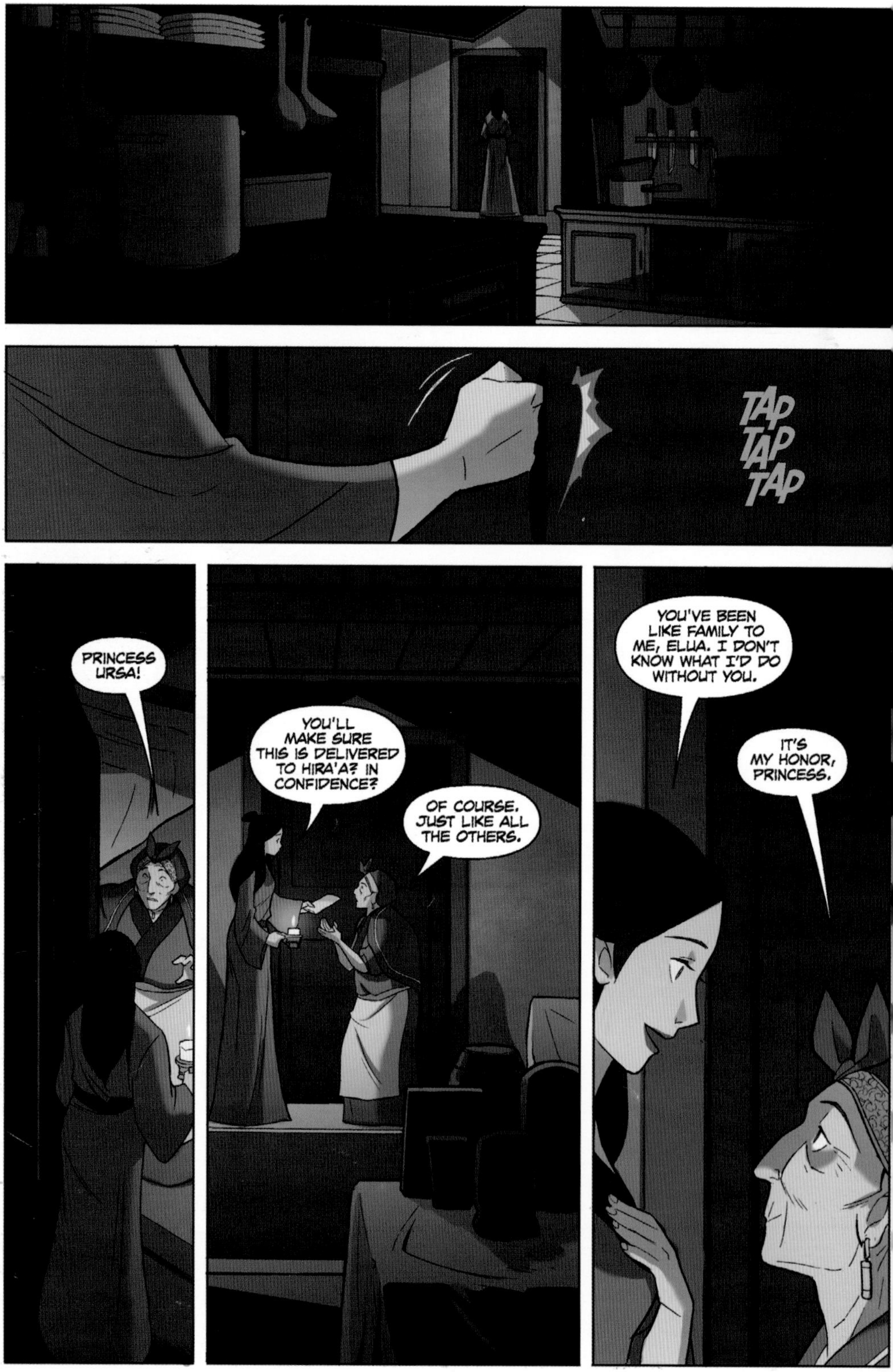
TAP
TAP
TAP
PRINCESS URSA!
YOU'LL MAKE SURE THIS IS DELIVERED TO HIRA'A? IN CONFIDENCE?
OF COURSE. JUST LIKE ALL THE OTHERS.
YOU'VE BEEN LIKE FAMILY TO ME, ELUA. I DON'T KNOW WHAT I'D DO WITHOUT YOU.
IT'S MY HONOR, PRINCESS.

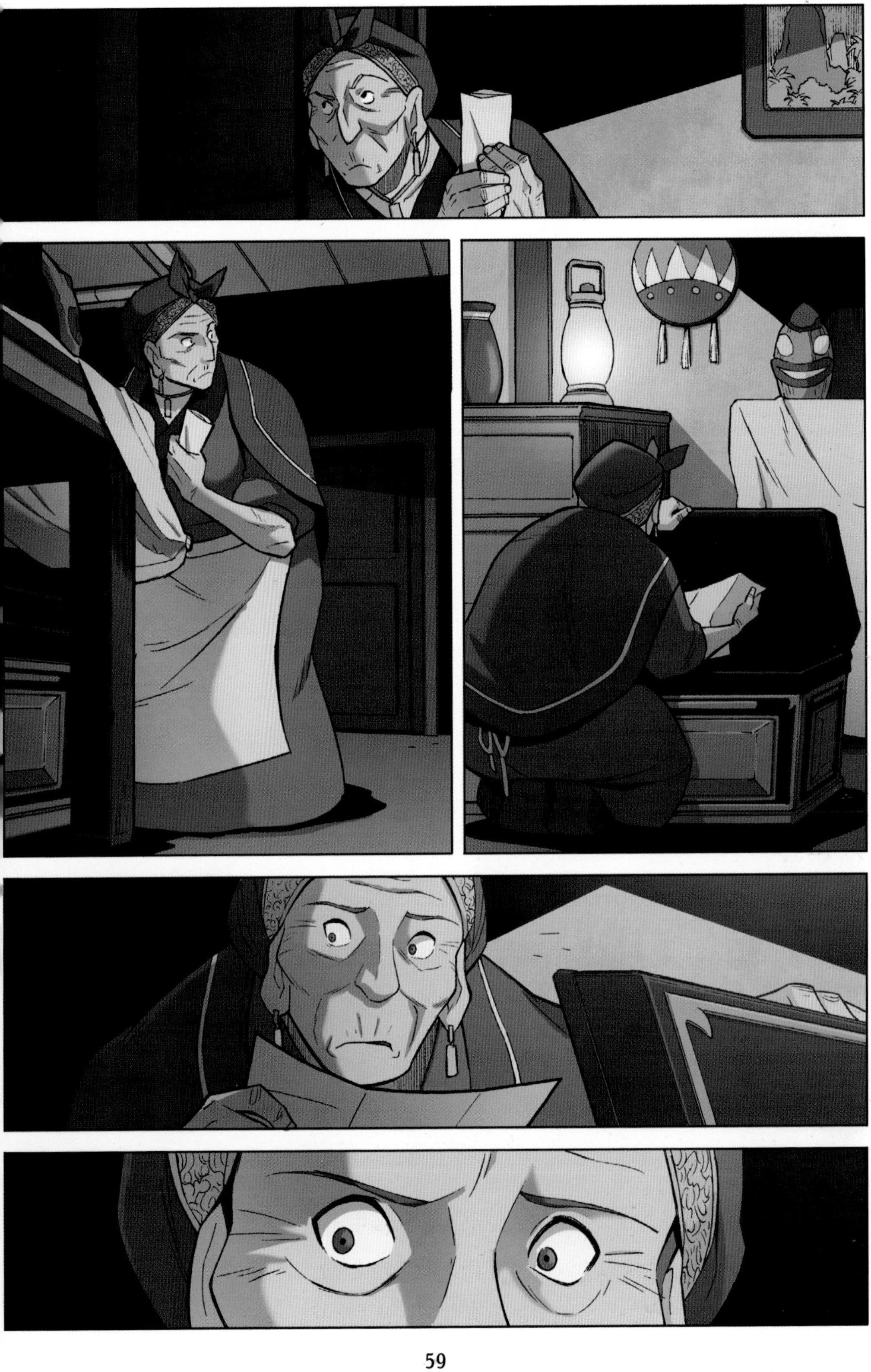

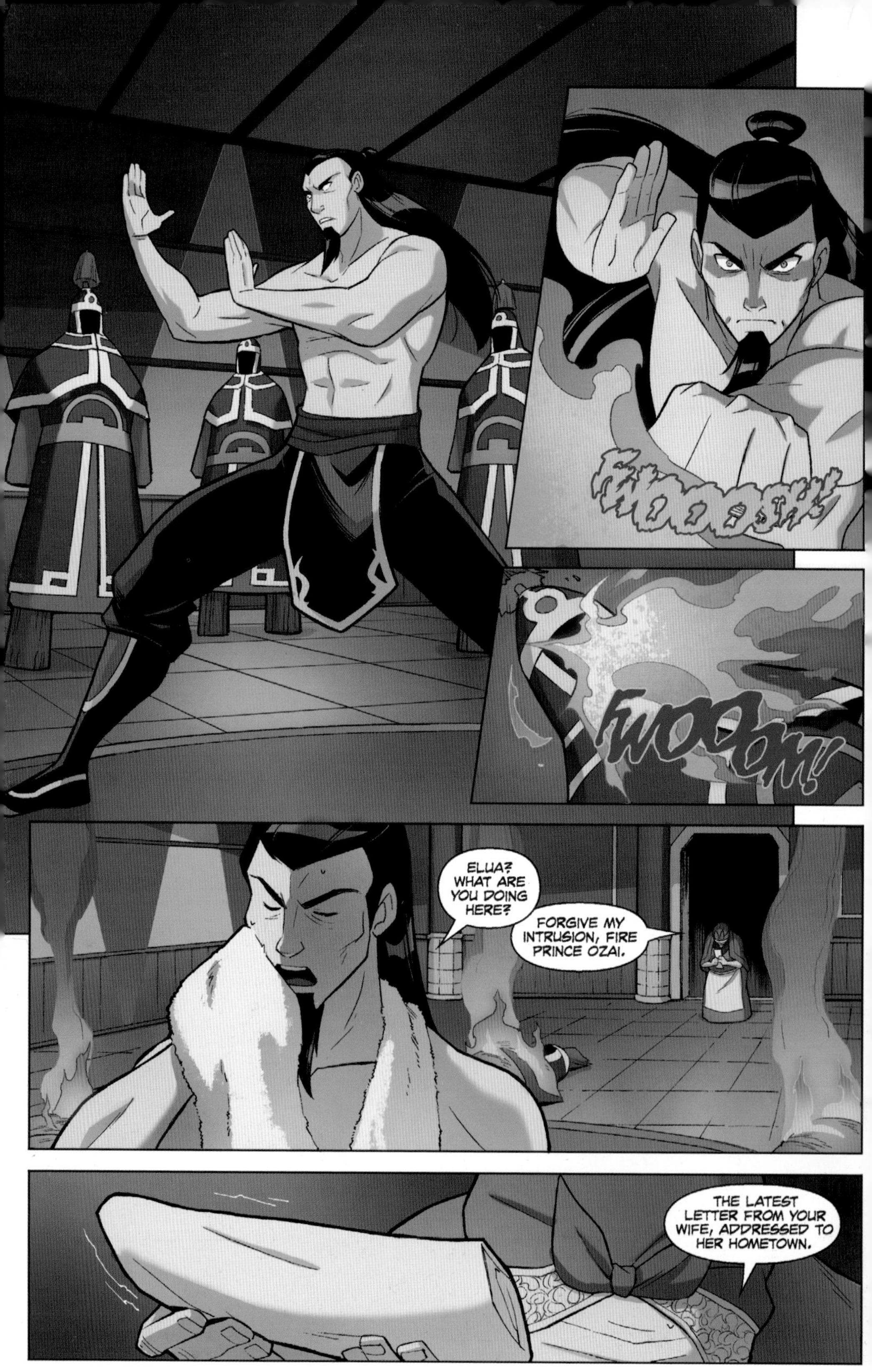
FWOOOSH!
FWOOOM!
ELUA? WHAT ARE YOU DOING HERE?
FORGIVE MY INTRUSION, FIRE PRINCE OZAI.
THE LATEST LETTER FROM YOUR WIFE, ADDRESSED TO HER HOMETOWN.

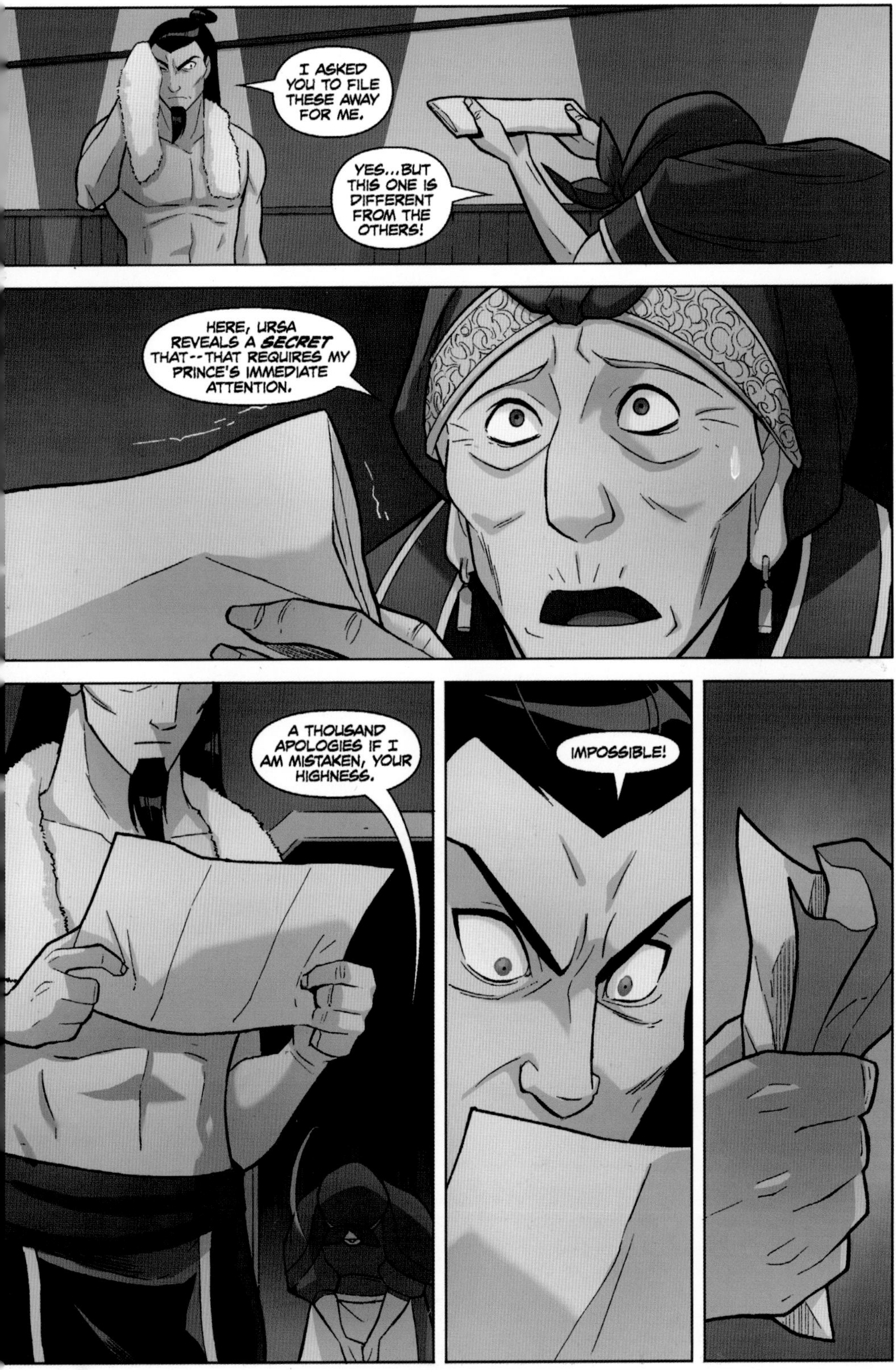
I ASKED YOU TO FILE THESE AWAY FOR ME.
YES...BUT THIS ONE IS DIFFERENT FROM THE OTHERS!
HERE, URSA REVEALS A *SECRET* THAT--THAT REQUIRES MY PRINCE'S IMMEDIATE ATTENTION.
A THOUSAND APOLOGIES IF I AM MISTAKEN, YOUR HIGHNESS.
IMPOSSIBLE!

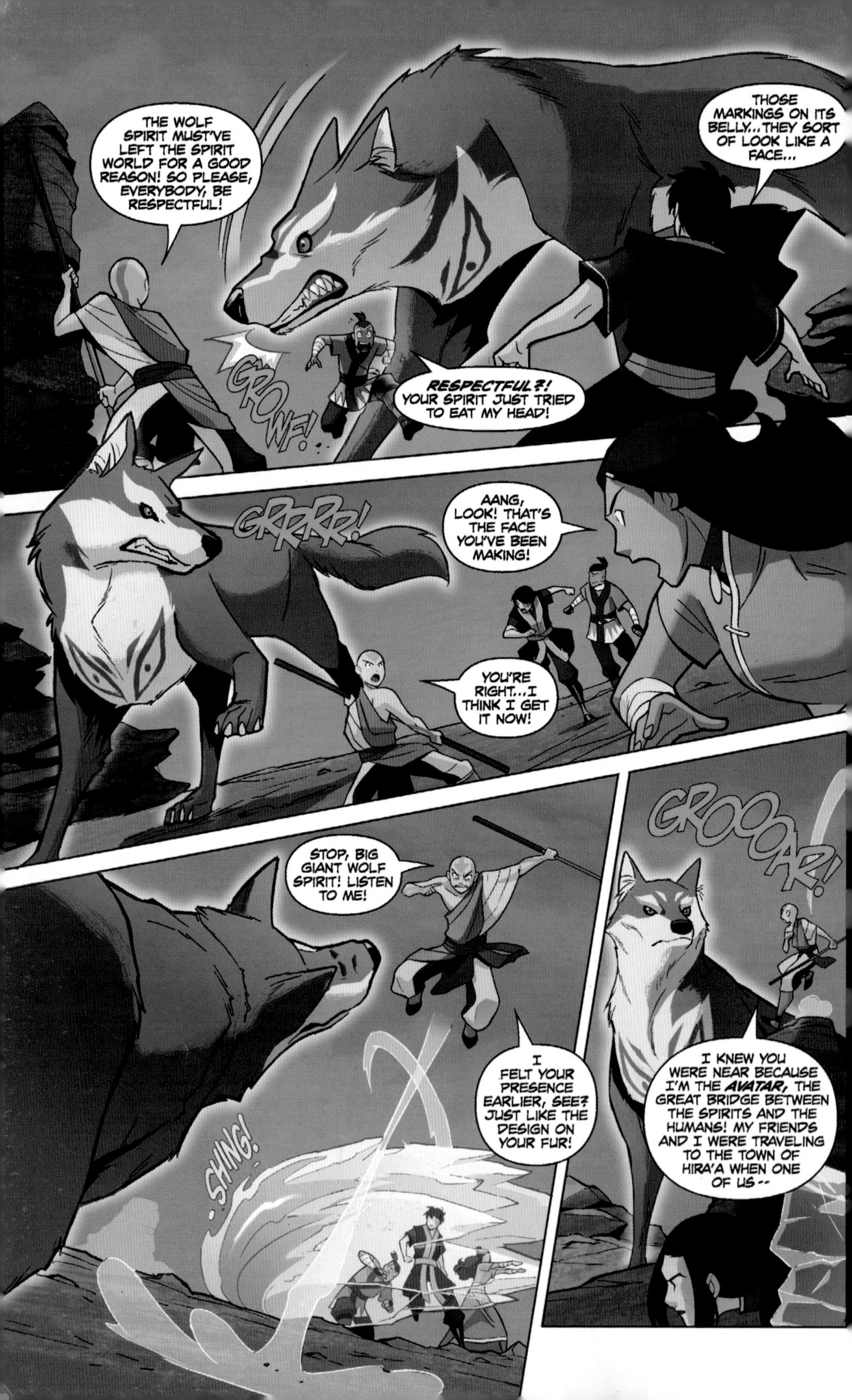
THE WOLF SPIRIT MUST'VE LEFT THE SPIRIT WORLD FOR A GOOD REASON! SO PLEASE, EVERYBODY, BE RESPECTFUL!
THOSE MARKINGS ON ITS BELLY...THEY SORT OF LOOK LIKE A FACE...
GROWF!
RESPECTFUL?! YOUR SPIRIT JUST TRIED TO EAT MY HEAD!
GRRRR!
AANG, LOOK! THAT'S THE FACE YOU'VE BEEN MAKING!
YOU'RE RIGHT...I THINK I GET IT NOW!
STOP, BIG GIANT WOLF SPIRIT! LISTEN TO ME!
I FELT YOUR PRESENCE EARLIER, SEE? JUST LIKE THE DESIGN ON YOUR FUR!
SHING!
GROOOAR!
I KNEW YOU WERE NEAR BECAUSE I'M THE AVATAR, THE GREAT BRIDGE BETWEEN THE SPIRITS AND THE HUMANS! MY FRIENDS AND I WERE TRAVELING TO THE TOWN OF HIRA'A WHEN ONE OF US--

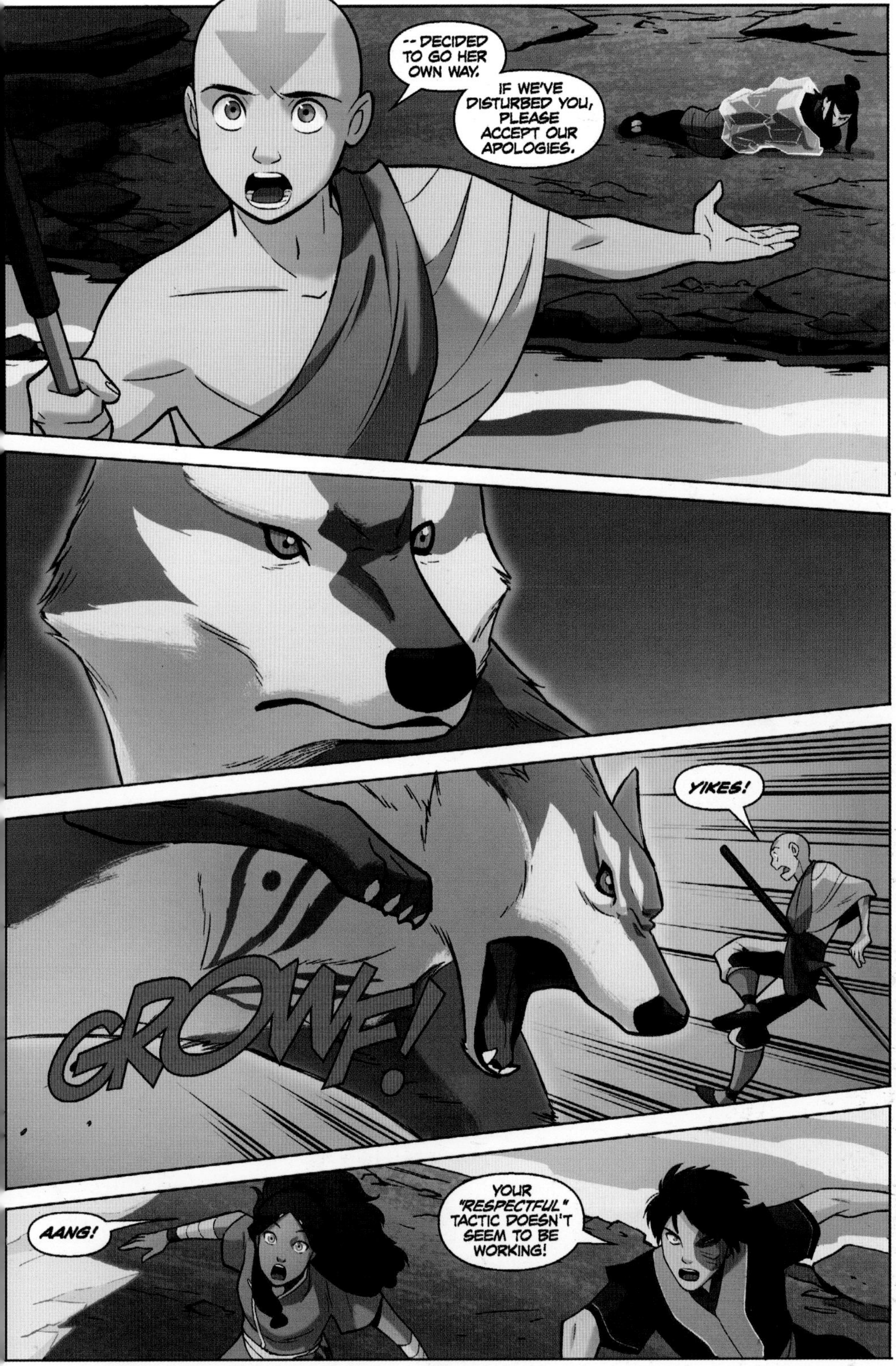
-- DECIDED TO GO HER OWN WAY.
IF WE'VE DISTURBED YOU, PLEASE ACCEPT OUR APOLOGIES.
YIKES!
GROWF!
AANG!
YOUR "RESPECTFUL" TACTIC DOESN'T SEEM TO BE WORKING!

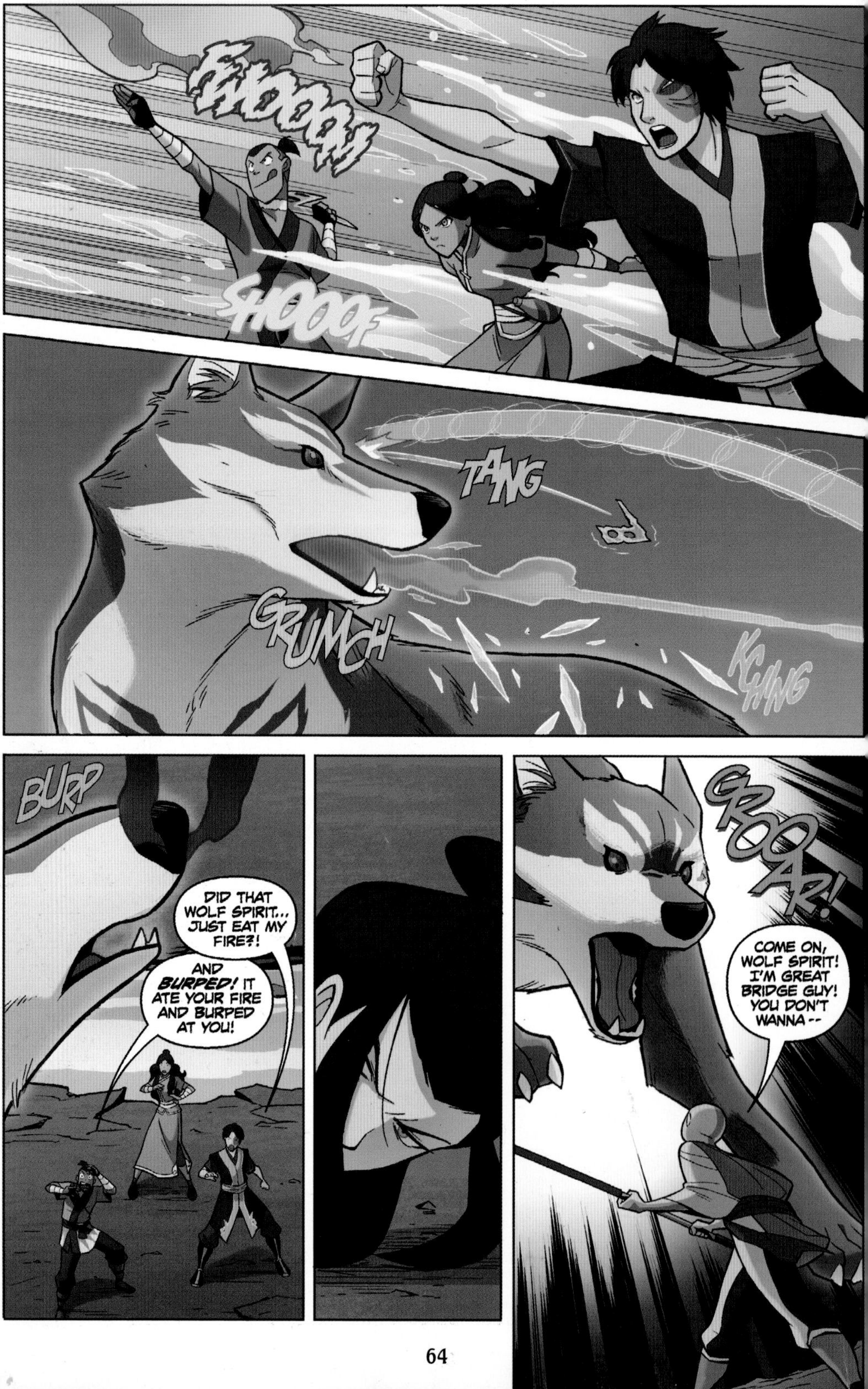

FWOOOSH
SHOOOF
TANG
CRUNCH
KCHING
BURP
DID THAT WOLF SPIRIT... JUST EAT MY FIRE?!
AND BURPED! IT ATE YOUR FIRE AND BURPED AT YOU!
GROOOAR!
COME ON, WOLF SPIRIT! I'M GREAT BRIDGE GUY! YOU DON'T WANNA --

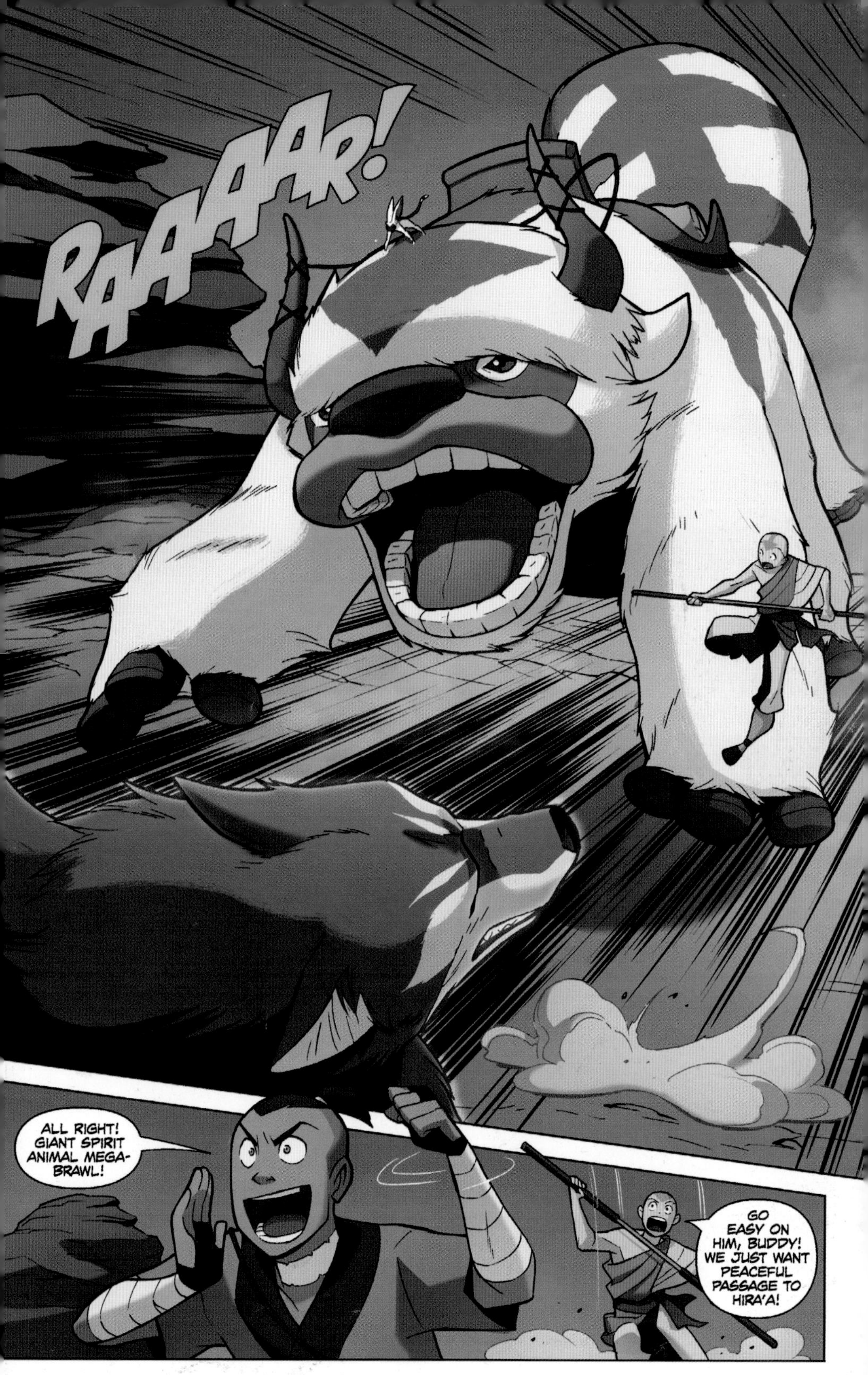
RAAAAAR!
ALL RIGHT! GIANT SPIRIT ANIMAL MEGA-BRAWL!
GO EASY ON HIM, BUDDY! WE JUST WANT PEACEFUL PASSAGE TO HIRA'A!

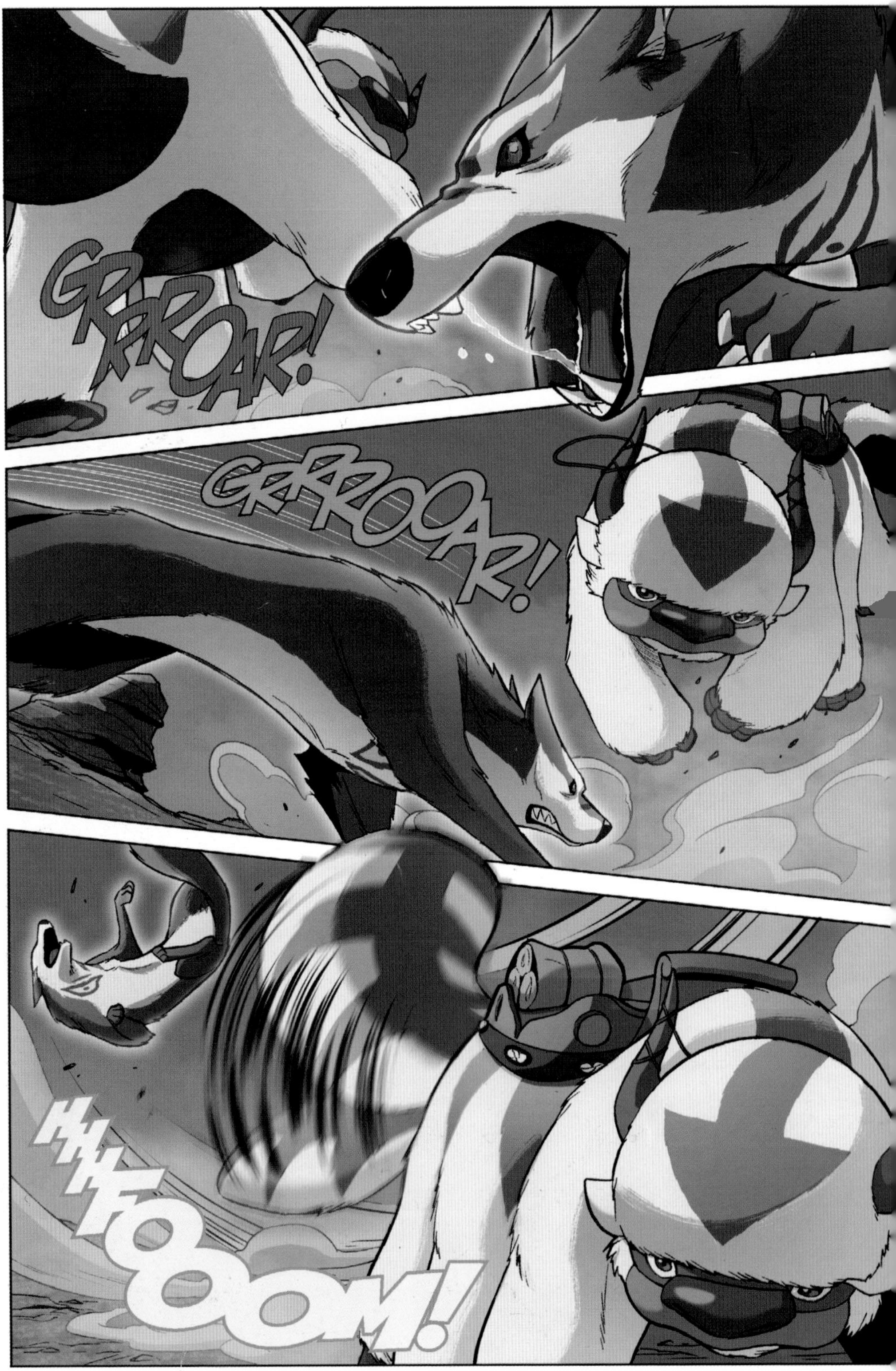
GRRROAR!
GRRROOAR!
HHFOOOM!

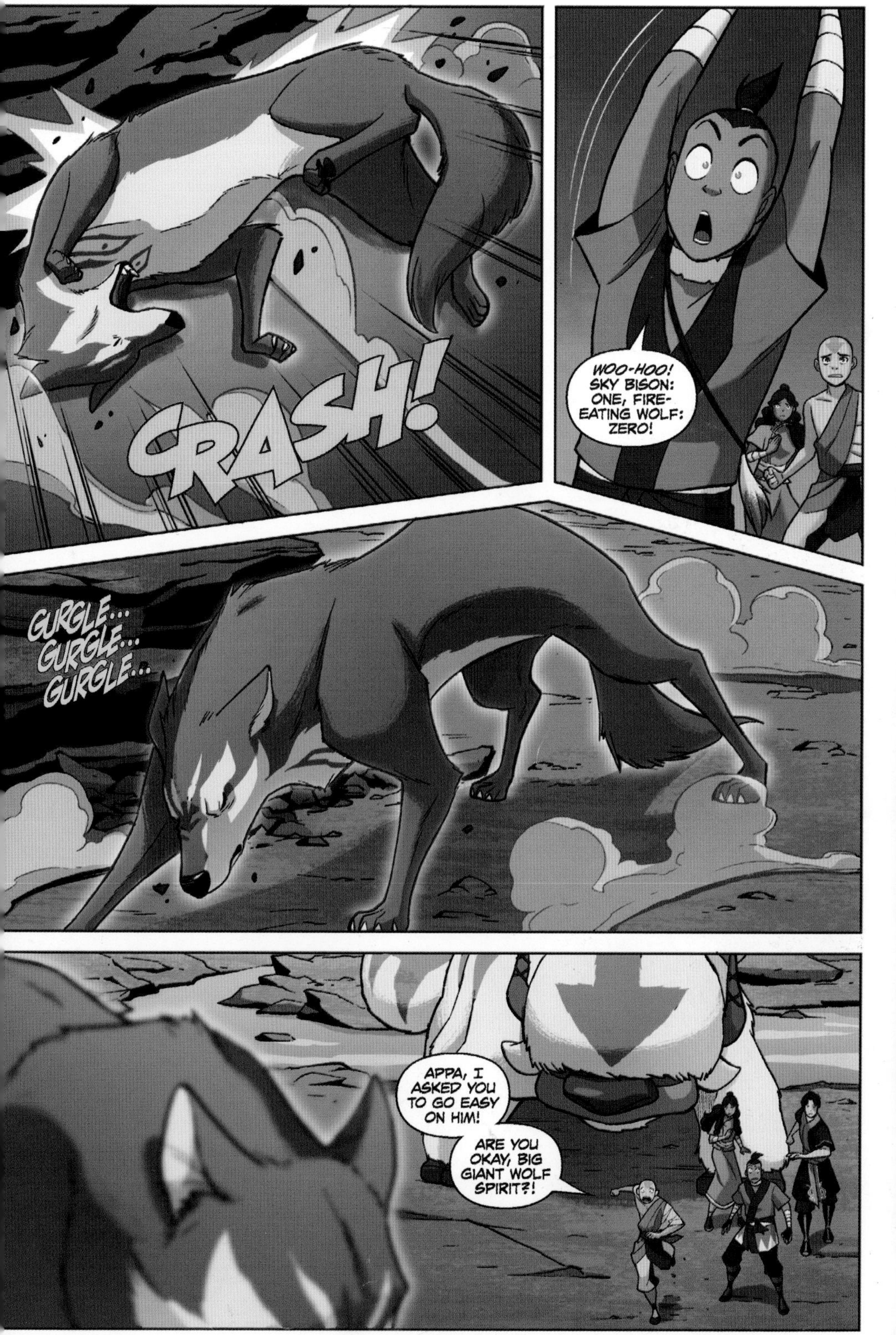
CRASH!
WOO-HOO! SKY BISON: ONE, FIRE-EATING WOLF: ZERO!
GURGLE... GURGLE... GURGLE...
APPA, I ASKED YOU TO GO EASY ON HIM!
ARE YOU OKAY, BIG GIANT WOLF SPIRIT?!

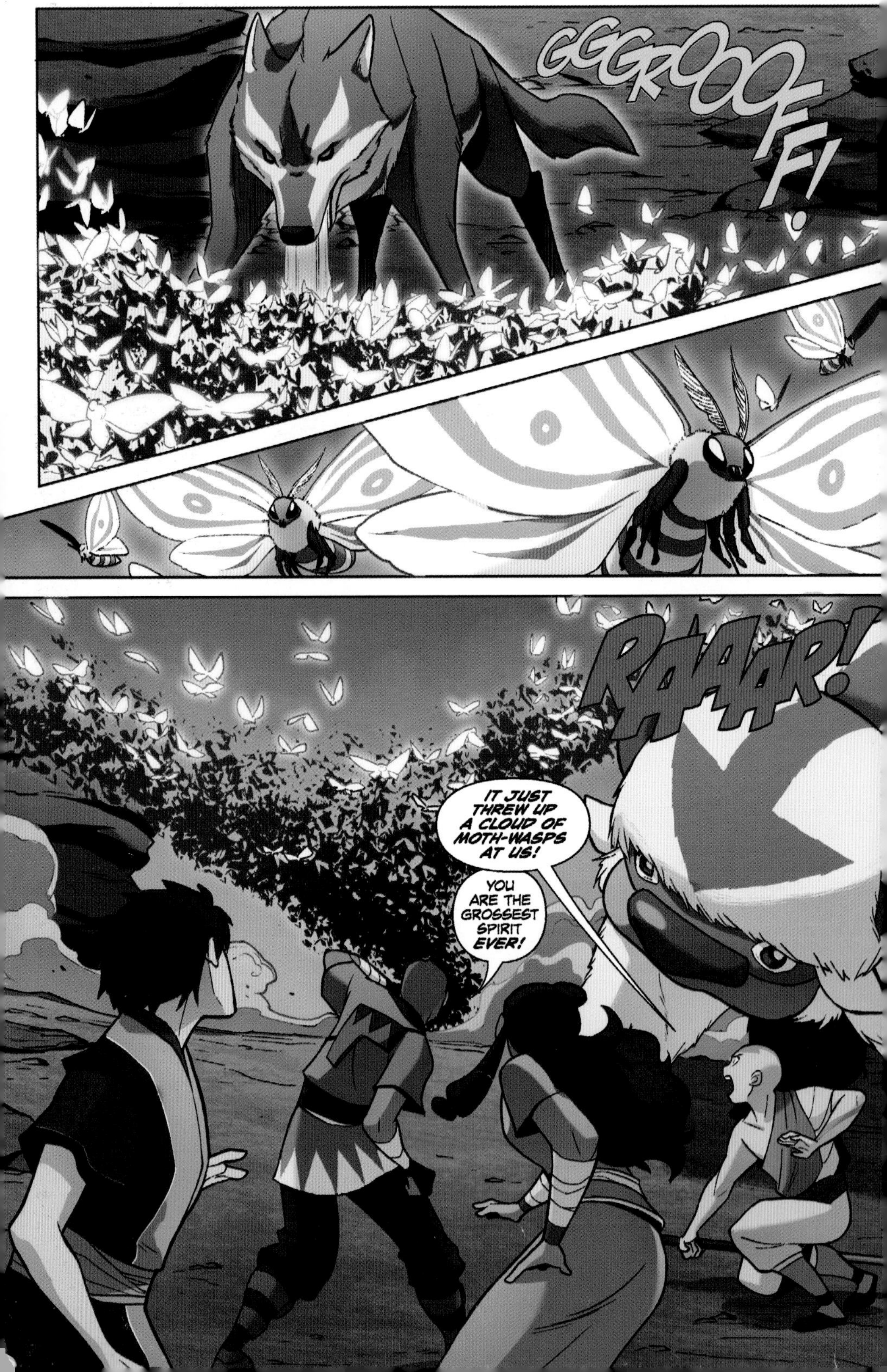
GGGROOOFF!
RAAAR!
IT JUST THREW UP A CLOUD OF MOTH-WASPS AT US!
YOU ARE THE GROSSEST SPIRIT EVER!

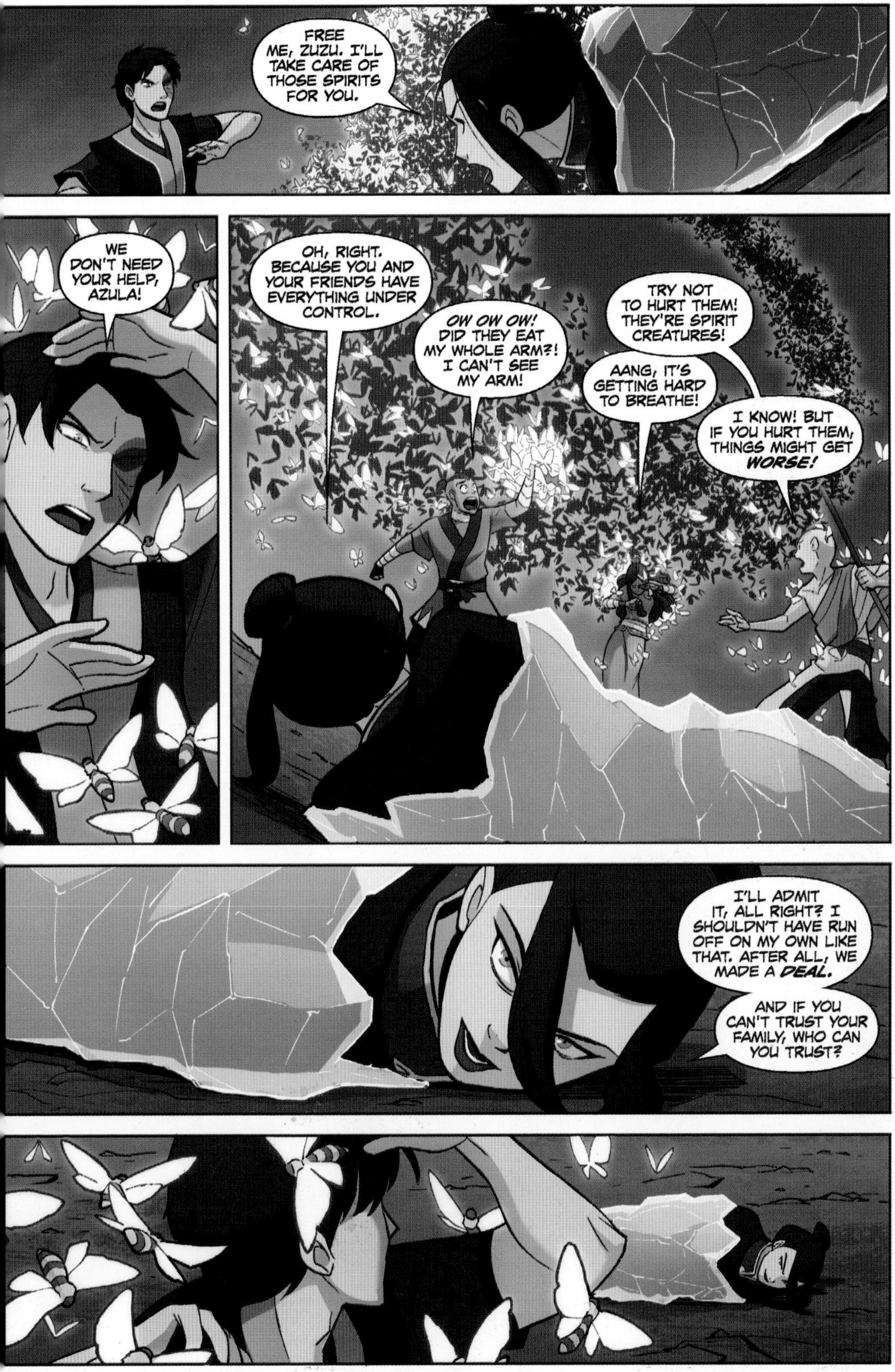
FREE ME, ZUZU. I'LL TAKE CARE OF THOSE SPIRITS FOR YOU.
WE DON'T NEED YOUR HELP, AZULA!
OH, RIGHT. BECAUSE YOU AND YOUR FRIENDS HAVE EVERYTHING UNDER CONTROL.
OW OW OW! DID THEY EAT MY WHOLE ARM?! I CAN'T SEE MY ARM!
AANG, IT'S GETTING HARD TO BREATHE!
TRY NOT TO HURT THEM! THEY'RE SPIRIT CREATURES!
I KNOW! BUT IF YOU HURT THEM, THINGS MIGHT GET WORSE!
I'LL ADMIT IT, ALL RIGHT? I SHOULDN'T HAVE RUN OFF ON MY OWN LIKE THAT. AFTER ALL, WE MADE A DEAL.
AND IF YOU CAN'T TRUST YOUR FAMILY, WHO CAN YOU TRUST?

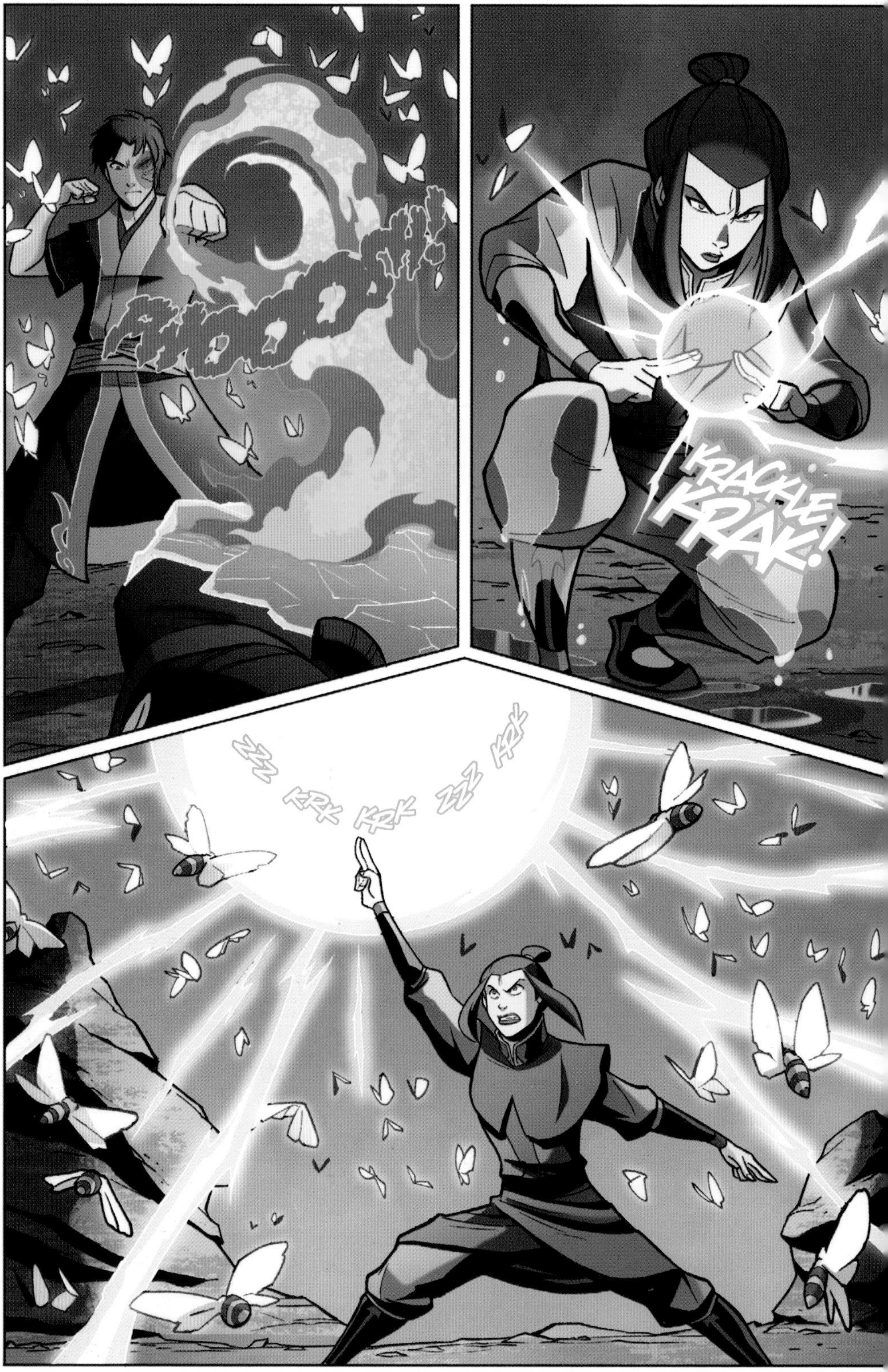
KRACKLE KRAK!
ZZZ KRK KRK ZZZ KRK

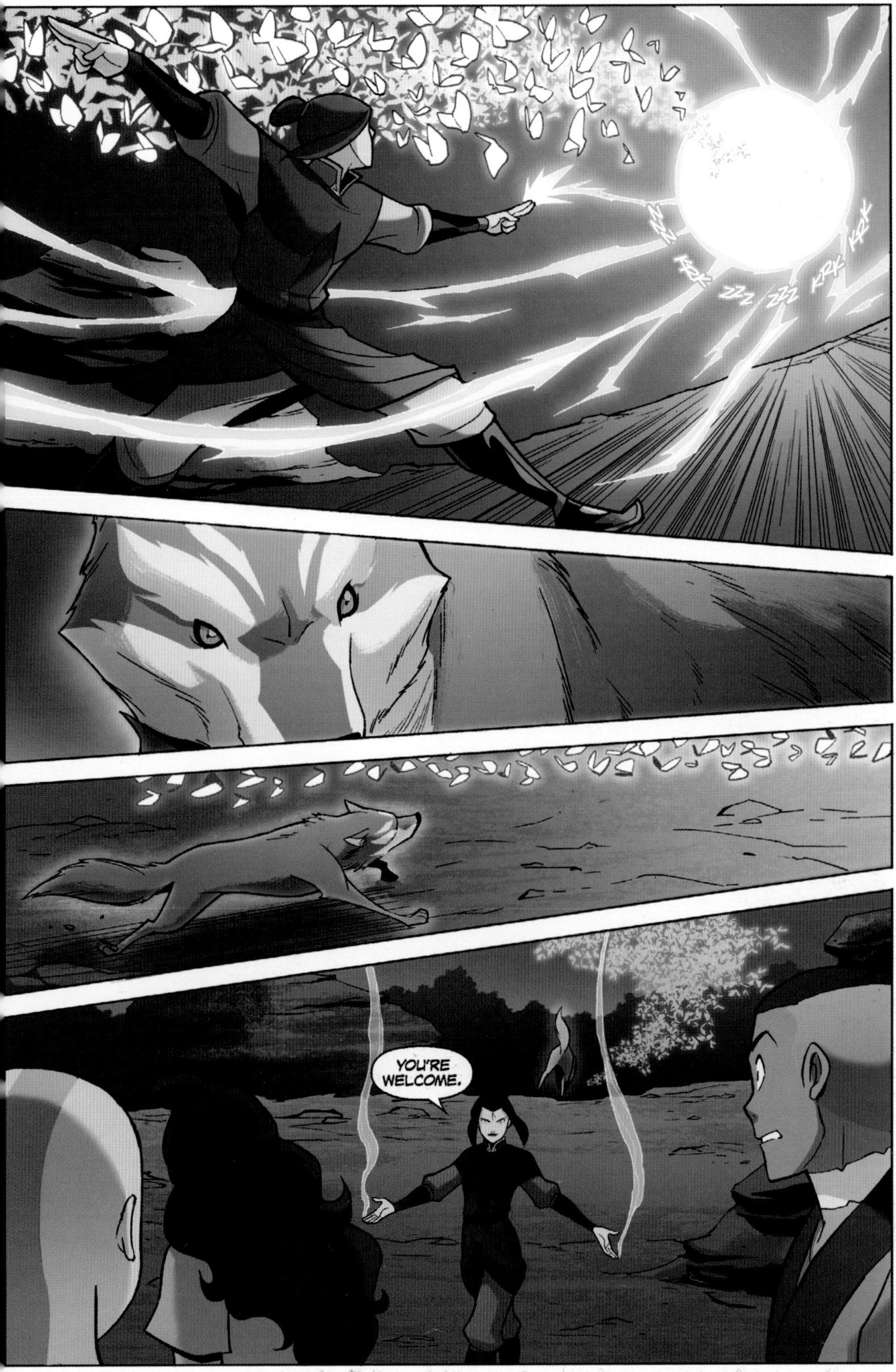
ZZZ
KRK
ZZZ
ZZZ
KRK
KRK
YOU'RE WELCOME.

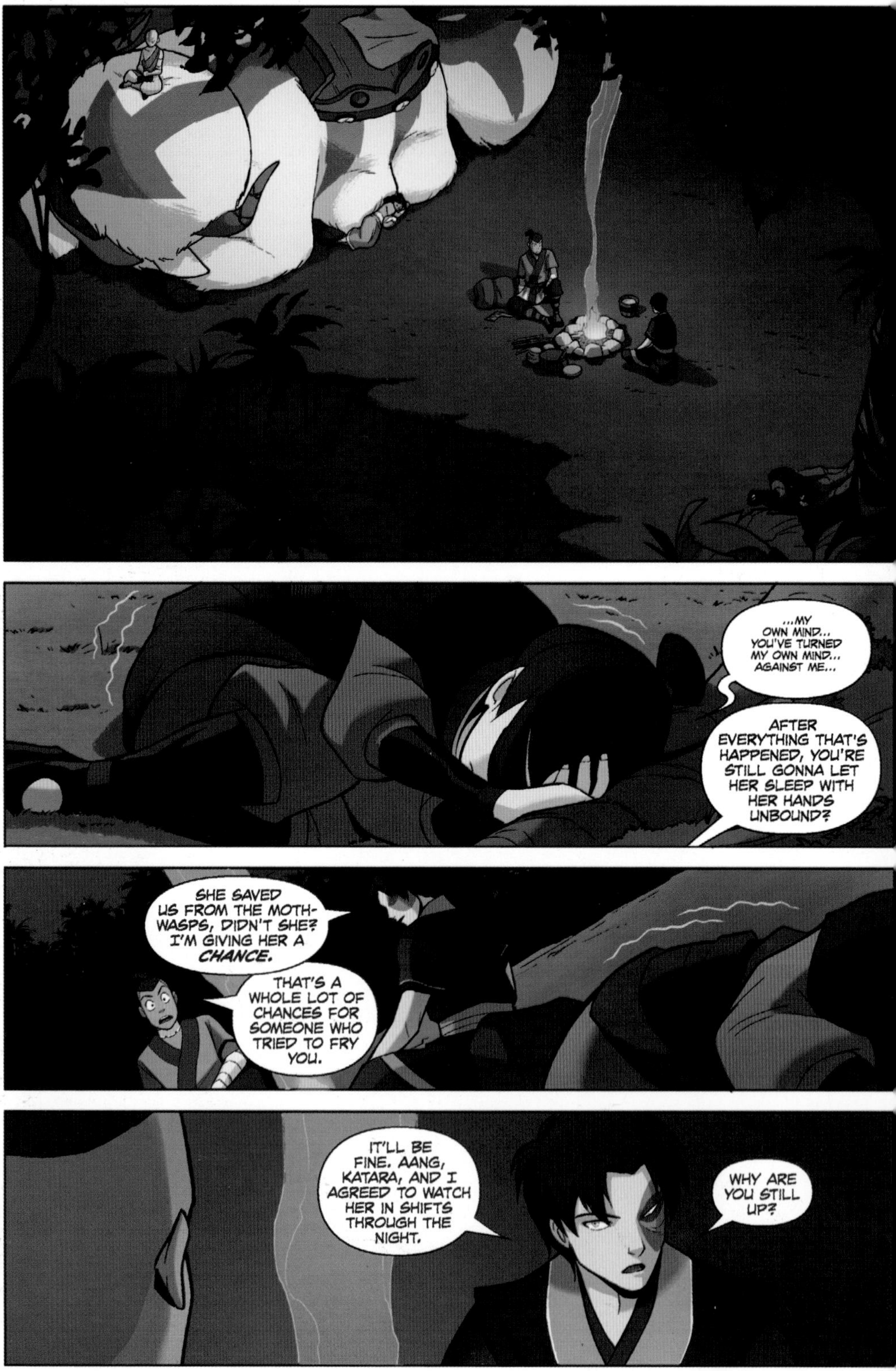
...MY OWN MIND... YOU'VE TURNED MY OWN MIND... AGAINST ME...
AFTER EVERYTHING THAT'S HAPPENED, YOU'RE STILL GONNA LET HER SLEEP WITH HER HANDS UNBOUND?
SHE SAVED US FROM THE MOTH-WASPS, DIDN'T SHE? I'M GIVING HER A CHANCE.
THAT'S A WHOLE LOT OF CHANCES FOR SOMEONE WHO TRIED TO FRY YOU.
IT'LL BE FINE. AANG, KATARA, AND I AGREED TO WATCH HER IN SHIFTS THROUGH THE NIGHT.
WHY ARE YOU STILL UP?

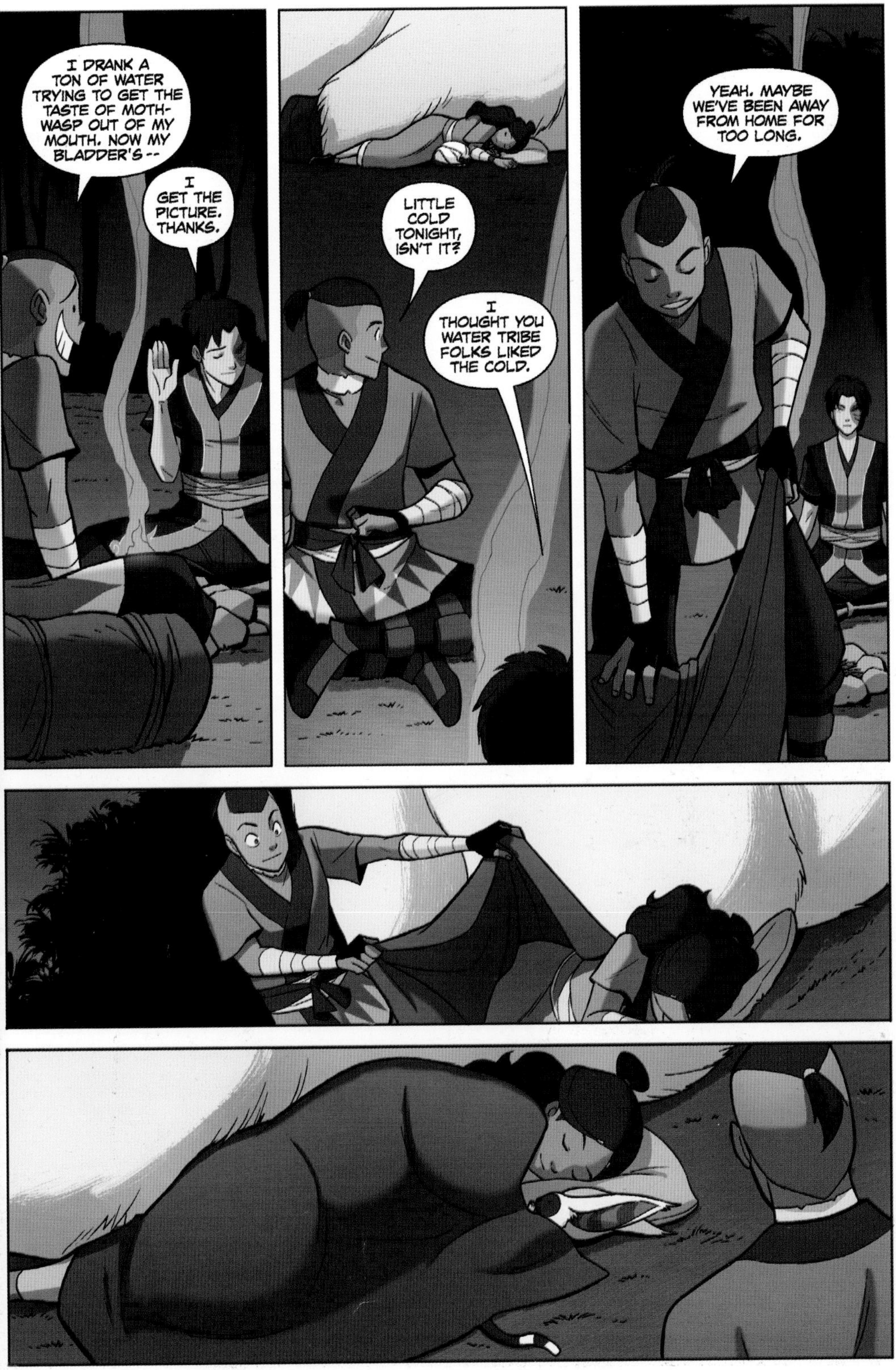
I DRANK A TON OF WATER TRYING TO GET THE TASTE OF MOTH-WASP OUT OF MY MOUTH. NOW MY BLADDER'S --
I GET THE PICTURE. THANKS.
LITTLE COLD TONIGHT, ISN'T IT?
I THOUGHT YOU WATER TRIBE FOLKS LIKED THE COLD.
YEAH. MAYBE WE'VE BEEN AWAY FROM HOME FOR TOO LONG.

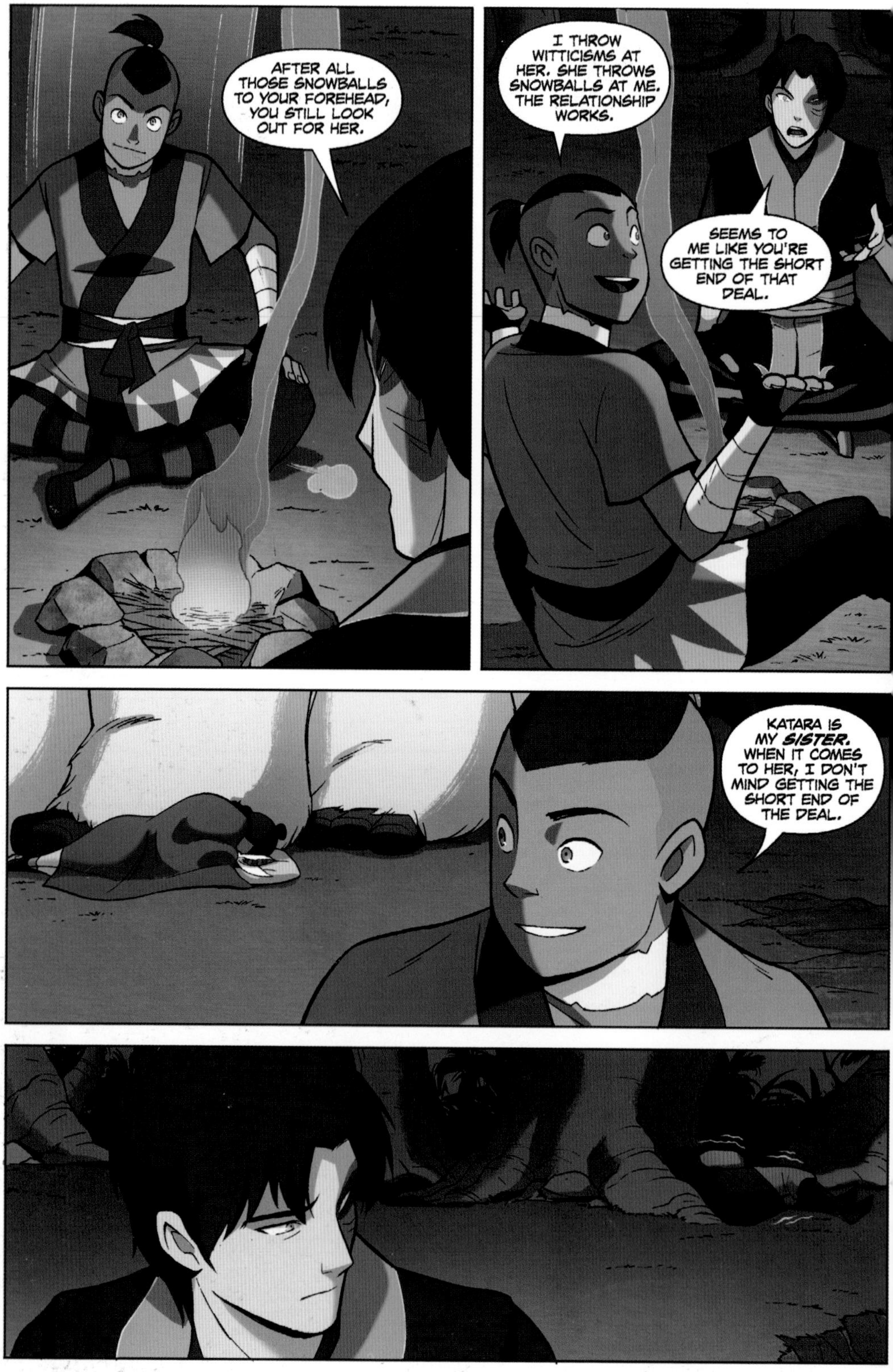
AFTER ALL THOSE SNOWBALLS TO YOUR FOREHEAD, YOU STILL LOOK OUT FOR HER.
I THROW WITTICISMS AT HER. SHE THROWS SNOWBALLS AT ME. THE RELATIONSHIP WORKS.
SEEMS TO ME LIKE YOU'RE GETTING THE SHORT END OF THAT DEAL.
KATARA IS MY *SISTER.* WHEN IT COMES TO HER, I DON'T MIND GETTING THE SHORT END OF THE DEAL.

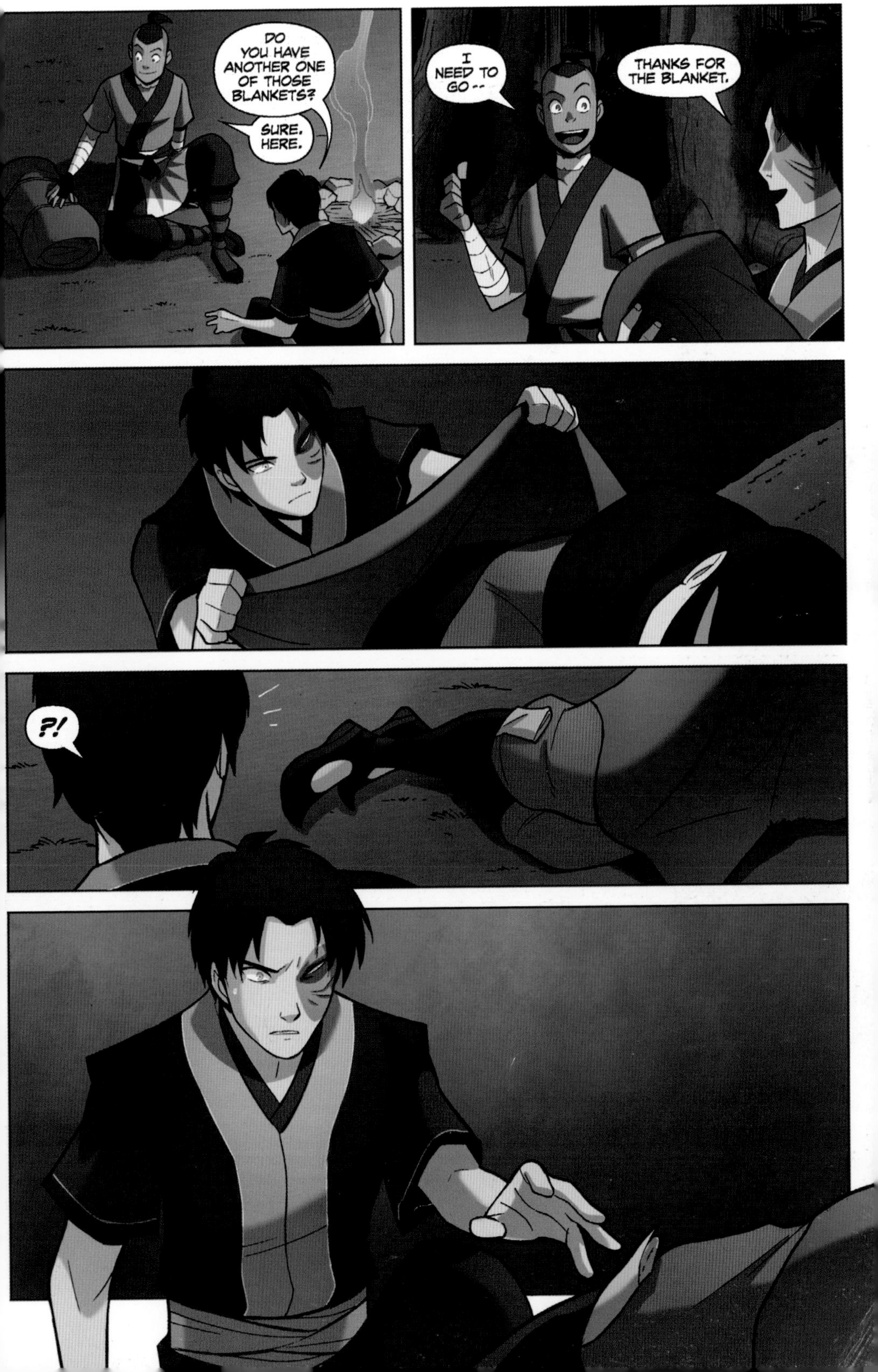
DO YOU HAVE ANOTHER ONE OF THOSE BLANKETS?
SURE. HERE.
I NEED TO GO --
THANKS FOR THE BLANKET.
?!

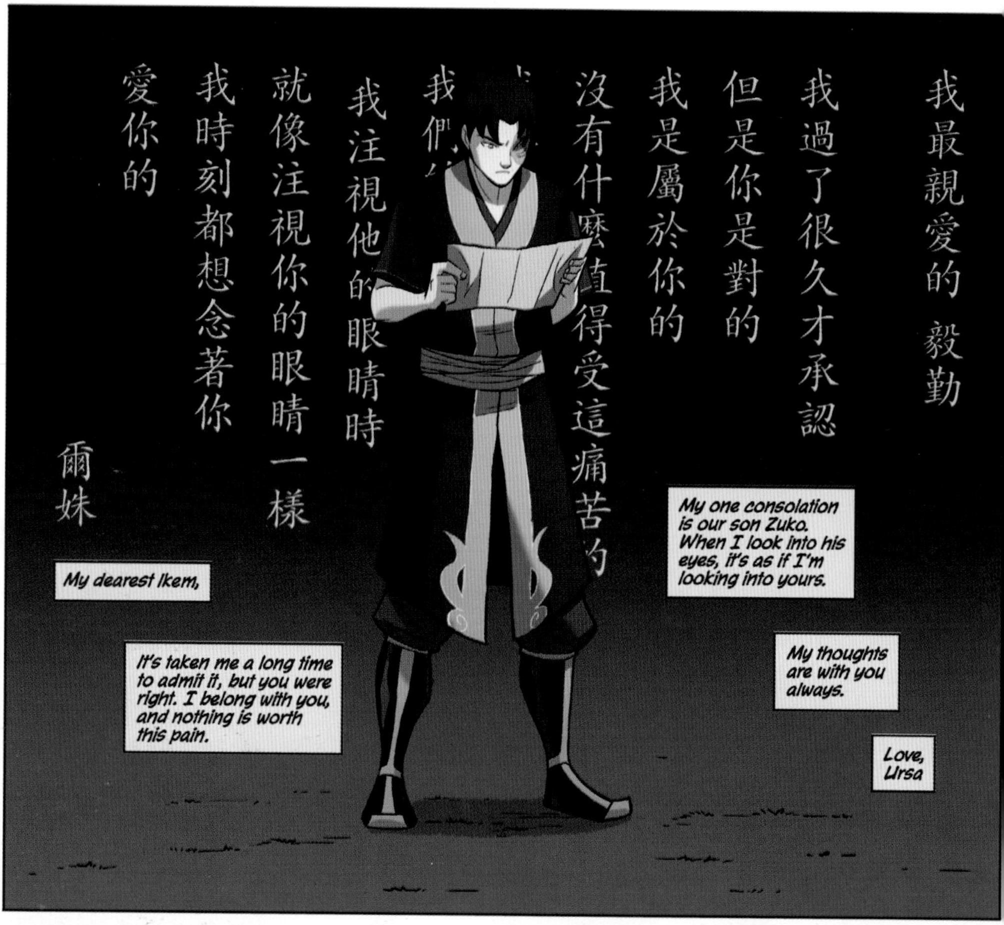
我最親愛的 毅勤
我過了很久才承認
但是你是對的
我是屬於你的
我注視他的眼睛時
就像注視你的眼睛一樣
我時刻都想念著你
愛你的
My dearest Ikem,
It's taken me a long time to admit it, but you were right. I belong with you, and nothing is worth this pain.
My one consolation is our son Zuko. When I look into his eyes, it's as if I'm looking into yours.
My thoughts are with you always.
Love, Ursa

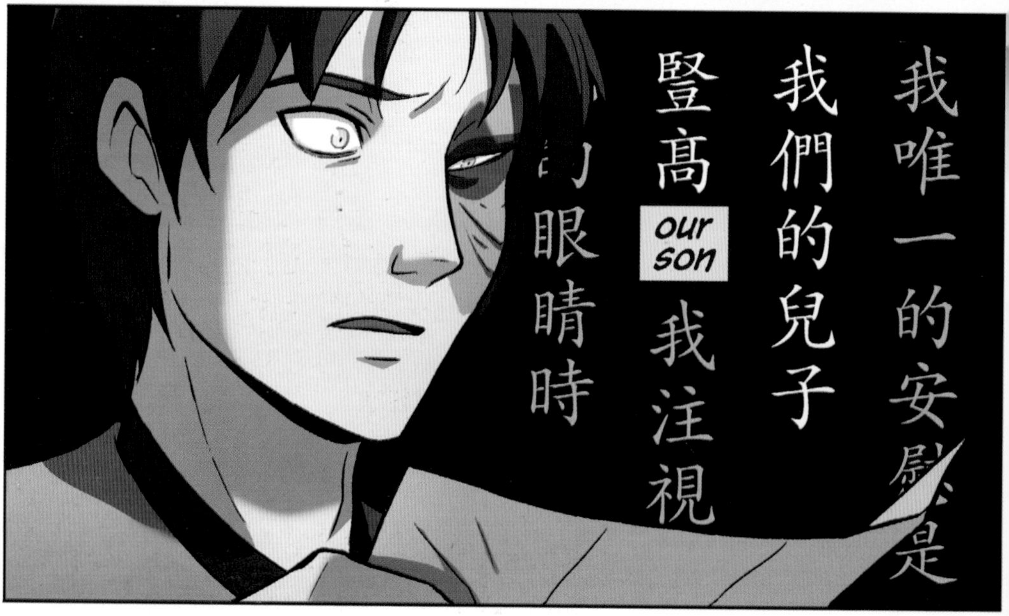
我們的兒子
our son
我注視

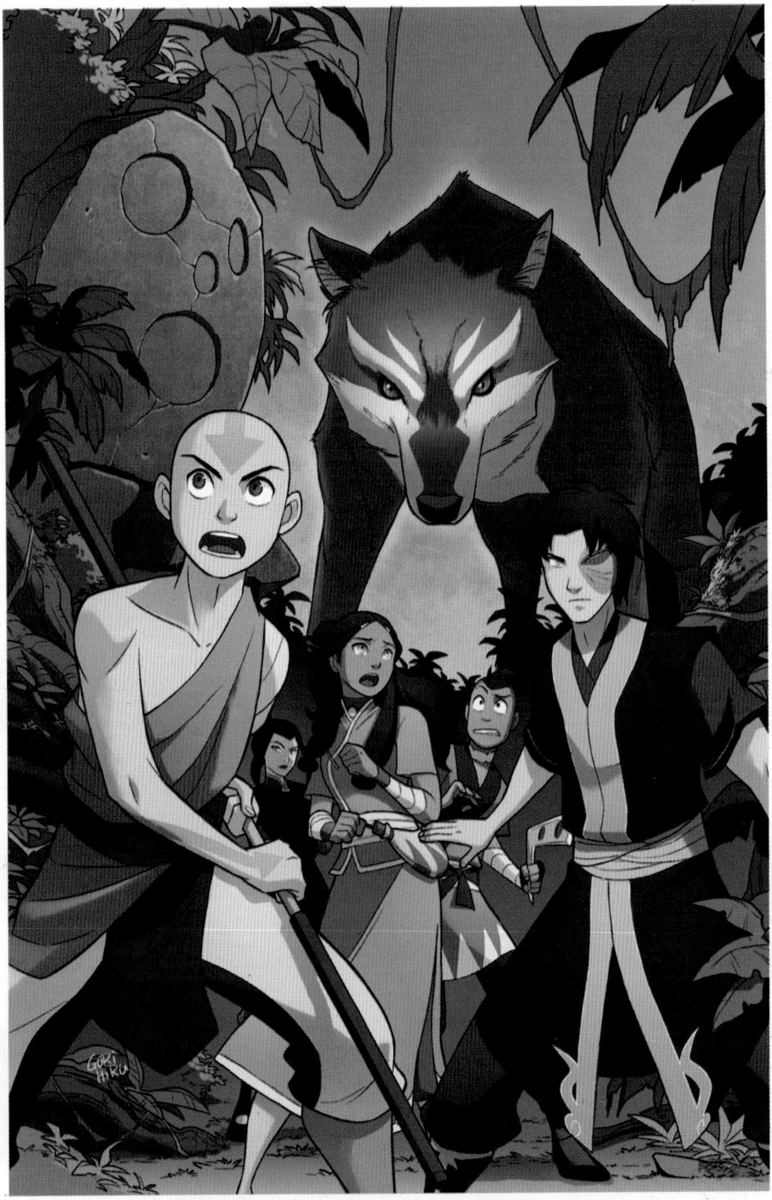

## COMING IN JULY

Zuko discovers the truth about his mother's past in . . .

**THE SEARCH · PART TWO**

# ALSO AVAILABLE FROM DARK HORSE BOOKS

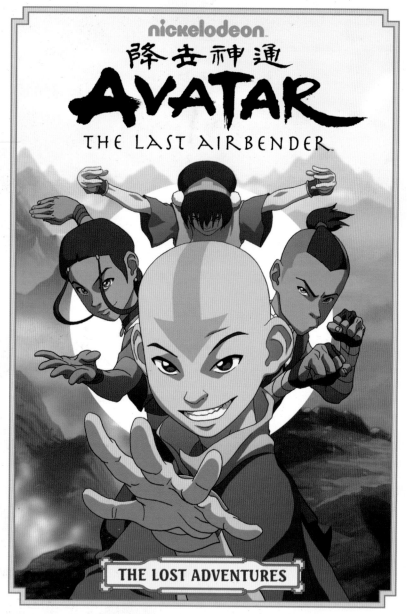

Twenty-eight stories set during the original three seasons, including over seventy pages of never-before-seen comics!

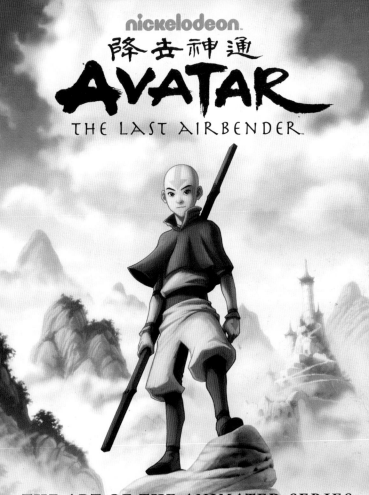